PRODUCTION Isn't Just

Don't confuse more time with more stuff or more status. We want to get more done because of what we can accomplish and become, not just for what we can have. When you hear the word production, don't just think of assembly lines or factories—that's just mechanical output. Production can be bigger, better, greater accomplishment in anything, including:

- **Teaching lessons—in the classroom or anywhere—that change lives**

- **Preparing quality meals**

- **Playing music that will lift and touch others**

- **Creating a pleasant and beautiful yard or garden**

- **Displaying determination and drive that inspires others**

- **Caring for children, the aged, or anyone well—making them comfortable and safe and happy—is one of the most productive things on earth**

Getting a lot done doesn't exclude the things that just give you enjoyment such as reading, picnicking, or taking pictures, either. Production isn't always tangible, but it always results in a recognizable change in something. A talk, poem, or deed that changes attitudes or behavior is wonderful production. Some very tangible results will usually follow.

What Will Happen When You Become a Go-Getter and Start Producing More?

- You'll be in demand, instead of being demanded on all the time!

- You'll have more time than you ever had before. (And, to think, some people try to find extra time by cutting down on what they're doing.)

- You'll know, no matter what life serves you up, you can't be cowed or defeated. No matter what happens, you still have worth.

- You'll have joy in the morning (and something to get up for!)

- You'll be absorbed in purposeful production, and success and happiness, all on their own, will sneak through a door you didn't know you'd left open.

- You'll know, maybe for the first time in your life, that you really matter. Having doubts as to whether you count—to your children, spouse, partner, boss, employees, or just in general as a human being is the number one source of unhappiness. If you know you matter then adversities, setbacks, and discouragements are only temporary inconveniences and slight irritations which you know you'll overcome.

When people are convinced that they make a difference, they make a difference.

Done!

How to Accomplish Twice as Much
in Half the Time–at Home and at the Office

2nd Edition

OTHER DON ASLETT BOOKS
FROM ADAMS MEDIA

Clutter's Last Stand, 2nd Edition

Do I Dust or Vacuum First?, 2nd Edition

The Office Clutter Cure, 2nd Edition

Pet Clean-Up Made Easy, 2nd Edition

Is There Life After Housework?, 2nd Edition

DONE!

How to Accomplish Twice as Much
in Half the Time–at Home and at the Office

2nd Edition

Don Aslett
America's #1 Cleaning Expert

Adams Media
Avon, Massachusetts

Published by
Adams Media, an F+W Publications Company
57 Littlefield Street, Avon, MA 02322. U.S.A.
www.adamsmedia.com

ISBN: 1-59337-507-7

Printed in Canada.

J I H G F E D C B A

Library of Congress Cataloging-in-Publication Data
Aslett, Don
Done! / Don Aslett.— 2nd ed.
p.   cm.
ISBN 1-59337-507-7
1. House Cleaning. 2. Time management. I. Title.

TX324.A75823 2005
648' .5--dc22   2005015476

This publication is designed to provide accurate and authoritative information with regard to the subject matter covered. It is sold with the understanding
that the publisher is not engaged in rendering legal, accounting, or other professional advice. If legal advice or other expert assistance is required, the services
of a competent professional person should be sought.

> From a *Declaration of Principles* jointly adopted by a
> Committee of the American Bar Association and a
> Committee of Publishers and Associations

Many of the designations used by manufacturers and sellers to distinguish their products are claimed as trademarks. Where those designations appear in this book and Adams
Media was aware of a trademark claim, the designations have been printed with initial
capital letters.

"Checklist for Action" pp. 150-152 © Carol Cartaino and Howard I. Wells.
Interior cartoon illustrations by jimhunt.us
Interior layout and design by Electronic Publishing Service, Inc. (TN)

This book is available at quantity discounts for bulk purchases.
For information, call 1-800-872-5627.

Contents

vii   Preface

1   Chapter One: Why Do More?

9   Chapter Two: Ordinary Me, Do More?

21   Chapter Three: A Little Subtraction . . .
          Adds a Lot of Production

53   Chapter Four: The Mainspring: Direction

85   Chapter Five: The Magic of Early

101   Chapter Six: How about Some Help?

137   Chapter Seven: Timepiece Tuners

167   Chapter Eight: The Healthy Stretch
          (Will It Hurt?)

197   Chapter Nine: The Rewards of Getting
          More DONE (Every Day!)

209   Index

Preface

Have you ever noticed how often people talk about not having enough time to get things done?

"Doesn't seem like I got much done today."

"Good grief, where did all the time go?"

"It couldn't be noon already, I just got started!"

"I didn't do half of what I intended this week."

"I've got enough to do for two lifetimes."

"If I could just skip sleeping, I might catch up."

"What I need is a forty-eight-hour day!"

We've all said things like this and we've heard them over and over from people in every type of situation. What we are really saying, of course, is:

||||||||||||||||||||||||||||||||||||||||||||||||||||||||||||||||||||||||||||||||||||||||||||||||

"I need *more time* to get things DONE!"

||||||||||||||||||||||||||||||||||||||||||||||||||||||||||||||||||||||||||||||||||||||||||||||||

Haven't we all attacked the time problem with every new approach and gadget around? Yet we *still* don't have enough time—or at least as much as we want. We all have a thousand things more to do than we're actually getting done.

Many of us have attempted, in vain, to stretch time, buy time, save time, stop time, find time, and beat time. We are even foolish enough to think we can *manage* time. Well, you can't do any of these things. You can't *make* time either—wow, what a commodity if you could just manufacture time and sell it!

There's only one alternative to losing time, wasting time, and trying to make up for lost time—it's the only thing we can really do with time, and that is **use it**! We can't manage time but we can manage our own behavior and activities to use time more wisely.

We'd all like to double our output in life, get forty-eight hours' worth out of the twenty-four. I meet thousands of people every year in my seminars, presentations, and media appearances, and no matter where I am, the purpose of the assemblage, or the assigned topic, the thing I'm most often asked is "How do you get so much done, Don?"

The answers in this book are my answers to getting more done, not a compilation of what two dozen other "how to beat the clock" books have to say. This is not the usual collection of sanctified information from Harvard or Yale, or the findings of fifty research assistants. I don't have secret formulas, a four-pound organization and scheduling workbook, or any chants or prayers to transform you into a super-doer. And I don't know all the answers. But I do have a proven track record, and I know from an ordinary, everyday standpoint how to get more done, every single day and week. When you produce more and get more out of your days, you become more valuable to yourself and to others. You become more needed and loved, and is there anything we want more than that?

Don Aslett

Doing more and being a go-getter doesn't mean making more money or scoring more points. It applies beyond "work" and business to every aspect of life—family, community, our social and religious activities, arts, and athletics. If we do more and better in anything, we will benefit. We all know that, and that's why everyone wants to know "How can I get more done?"

Acknowledgments

People often wonder how I get so much done, but I don't wonder. I know I've been blessed with not just energy and enthusiasm but more than my share of people who've taught me a thing or two, and people who have inspired me to stretch, seek, and use everything I have to find better ways to do things.

Notable among these are:

My father, Duane Aslett, master of management and accomplishment. He did it on the roads and farm fields of the West, but he could have done it anywhere.

The thousands of women across the country I've been privileged to meet in my life, in the course of my seminars and presentations, and through the mail—especially the mothers, who can outproduce most of us with one hand tied behind them.

My many business clients and colleagues including the Bell System and Mark Browning.

Tobi Flynn, my general manager, expediter extraordinaire, and a model of accomplishment in her own right.

And my editor and collaborator Carol Cartaino, who can pull ideas out of me I didn't realize I had, give me new thoughts and inspirations, and (sometimes against all odds) pull it all together smoothly.

Chapter 1
Why Do More?

Just or not, like it or not, there seems to be a pretty clear ranking of people according basically to how much they can get done. "Doing" draws a dividing line quicker and surer than anything you'll ever see. And the super-doers have an advantage, a deserved advantage, over the regular run of humankind.

The *go-getters,* those who do more, are the people most desired and admired—it's that simple. The world rewards them the most, bosses hire and pay them the most, and they even seem to have the most fun. Average people get treated average. The high producers, the doers, get treated the best, and it's only fair and logical that they should. Those who do the most *should* get the most.

If you have any doubts about this, since we believe in the democratic system, let's vote on it!

If we were only allowed a one-word epitaph, I'd want mine to be "Productive." "Generous," "kind," "rich," and "reverent" are nice, too, but all of the above are easily or potentially included in "productive."

The following are some of the main reasons for doing more. If you agree with each of these and/or would like to have that advantage, vote yes. If not, check no.

Official Ballot: **Why Do More?**

Yes No

○ ○ **To find genuine self-respect.** We always know, deep down, whether we're accomplishing anything or not. And no external pleasure can beat the inner satisfaction of knowing we can do it, that we DID it!

○ ○ **To avoid passenger status.** Doing more will put you in the driver's seat—you can get behind the wheel and go where and when you want to go. The average achiever generally has to be content to be hauled wherever others want to take him.

○ ○ **For a better job.** Production is what every employer is looking for. Production is valuable and people who produce are promoted and well paid as well as praised.

○ ○ **So you *qualify*.** Notice how for many things in life—a license, a loan, a job, a policy, a school, a team, a race, or a mortgage—we have to qualify before we are accepted. In our everyday lives, in a more subtle way, we do exactly the same thing with others—we qualify them before we decided to love or want them.

○ ○ **For family strength! For better relationships.** Many divorces are a result of the fact that one of the parties is a nonproducer. They don't produce a living, a pleasing personality, a positive example for the kids, a feeling of companionship and appreciation, etc.

○ ○ **To have more choices and not be left to chance as much.** The achiever has more options, period—in jobs, positions, locations, even potential mates. The achiever is not relying on the luck of the draw for success. He or she is going out and making it happen.

○ ○ **Because high production is a great communicator.** Many things are misunderstood because they were written or said wrong, but actions come across clearly. When something is done (not planned, promised, or intended, but DONE), little has to be said or explained or evaluated—the act speaks for itself.

○ ○ **Because a day *will* come when you'll have to do more.** You may face a financial bind or stepped-up competition in your business or profession, suddenly be in charge of a company, a project, a field trip, or a family . . . or have two sets of twins. If you know how to do more, you'll handle it well and even enjoy it; if you don't, you'll experience frustration, disappointment, and failure rather than rewards.

○ ○ **For attention, all-eyes-on-you attention! Average may get an honorable mention, but producers get our full attention.** It's the doer, the leader, the inventor, the explorer we all want to hear about. If you do a lot, you'll have an unmistakable identity.

○ ○ **To have influence.** Because you become a number-setter instead of just a number, you count instead of being counted. You make a difference in life and society. We quickly lose interest in people who don't contribute. People not only love producers, they listen to them.

○ ○ **Leverage! We so often use the wrong tools to get our way, to influence others, to get a raise, a transfer, a sale—we try politics, payoffs, begging, bullying, and other inferior approaches, all taking time and effort and resulting in a doubtful outcome.** Higher production is the greatest leverage in the world. Real producers can name their price and place and write their own tickets.

○ ○ **For that elusive thing called security.** I love General Douglas MacArthur's definition of security: *The ability to produce.* As long as you can and do produce, you have security. Job security, for example, is a darn good reason to do more. You don't want to be one of those thinned from the ranks when the thinning starts. Few bosses or company owners will let a productive person go.

○ ○ **So that you will expand as you grow older, not diminish.** So many people spend all their time looking forward to retirement, to their *withdrawal* from production. But age seasons us into, not out of, our best productive years. When we're older we have more to give and teach, we're more qualified to guide, direct, and advise. If you want an exciting life, you have to keep putting out the effort to do exciting things, until you're 95 or 105! If you retire from production, everyone (except those who are after your money) will gradually retire from you.

○ ○ **For the carryover—productivity will aid and improve every area of your life! Once you master the principles of getting lots done in one area, the same laws and like principles will apply to other situations.** This is why people who move mountains in one area often seem to have a golden touch for other things. That is carryover.

○ ○ **For the financial rewards.** People who do more profit economically as well as physically and emotionally. There is a tough, but true, lesson most of us have learned by now—we aren't rewarded for just wandering around in life. Those who do more, get more!

○ ○ **Productive people are almost irresistible—they attract others and draw respect, help, cooperation, and opportunities from all sides.** Their very presence creates energy that draws the good deals. Think for a minute of the things, people, and events that impact and influence you the most. We love the car that goes the fastest, the garden soil and fruit trees that yield the most and best. It's the doer we all love, because working hard and producing a lot brings out all of the knowledge and passion in a person.

○ ○ **To give yourself a real sense of purpose.** The do-too-muchers are often happier and less depressed than the never-do-enoughers. Knowing you are doing something that matters is a big, if not **THE** biggest, motivating factor in the world.

○ ○ **To cut waste.** People who spend more time achieving don't have the time, space, or desire to stockpile "junk" or useless things. When you're doing more you don't have time for excess spending or getting into trouble.

○ ○ **You'll at last be able to keep your output up with your imagination! You won't be carrying around twenty pages of things "to do someday" anymore, because a great many of them will be done! Think of that.**

○ ○ **It's the right thing to do.** Our very existence takes up space, wears things out, and uses up food and energy. Helping, doing our share to replace, replenish, and rebuild things is an obligation we all have. It's our **duty** to produce a lot!

○ ○ **It takes you out of average.** Neither you nor anyone else really wants or seeks out the average and ordinary. Do you go fishing for the smallest fish? Want to read the average book or see the average movie? Do you want an average job or an average mate? Do you say at payday, "Oh, just give me the average?" It's human nature to want to excel, and to love those who excel. In all of life's pursuits—office to university, baseball field to bedroom—people want and expect **the best**. Average isn't bad—but you don't have to settle for it!

If you voted Yes on eleven or more of these ballot options, then you have good reason to read on. If you haven't voted Yes on many of these options, then you have even better reasons to keep reading.

The Best Part of Getting More DONE

Let me sum up this production business now with the bottom line of life, which is basically two things: to love and to be loved. If you can achieve these two things, the other 10,000 needs and wants will follow. It feels SO good to be loved and needed. Being cared about is the greatest pleasure and experience on the face of the earth. It never gets old and we can't have too much of it. What does it really take to be loved? **Production**! We pity, tend to, and tolerate depressed, tired, "ordinary effort" people—we don't *love* them.

As for that equally important business of *loving*, what other measuring stick is there for it if not what and how much we do? Looks? Talk? Position? Money in the bank? Promises? Intentions? We can have all of these and still be worthless and undesirable. Love is **doing**, not just feeling.

Production Isn't Just Mechanical Output

Don't confuse more time with more stuff or more status. We want to get more done because of what we can accomplish and become, not just what we can have.

When you hear the word *production*, don't just think of assembly lines—that's just mechanical output. Production can be bigger, better, greater accomplishment in anything:

- Teaching lessons—in the classroom or anywhere—that change lives
- Preparing quality meals

- Playing music that will lift and touch others
- Creating a pleasant and beautiful yard or garden
- Displaying determination and drive that inspires others
- Caring well for children, the aged, or anyone, making them comfortable and safe and happy—this is one of the most productive things on earth

Getting a lot done doesn't exclude the things that just give you enjoyment such as reading, picnicking, or taking pictures, either. Production isn't always tangible, but it always results in a recognizable change in something. A talk, poem, or deed that changes attitudes or behavior is wonderful production. Some very tangible results will usually follow.

Getting More DONE Is the Most Direct Route to What You're Looking For!

It's the answer to most of our problems. It gives us self-esteem, satisfaction, a sense of purpose, and a good livelihood. Production keeps us in touch, in focus, in demand, in charge, and interesting (not to mention **in income**!). Production generates more self-worth, security, and personal value than any other single alternative.

So let's *do* something! Lots!

Chapter 2

Ordinary Me, Do More?

Every book needs a Little Engine That Could chapter, and this is it. This is the answer to the question that's forming in your mind right now: "But can plain old ordinary me do more?"

Too many people believe that they have to be or know some kind of efficiency expert to use time better. They're convinced that you have to attend a seminar, gain a college degree, lug around a thick calendar planner, or use a PDA to master the magic of MORE . . . This is, without a doubt, absolutely not true!

There are those out there who try to make a mystery out of time efficiency. There is none, nor is it difficult. Your time IQ is equal to anyone's, whether you're a bank clerk from Boston, personal assistant from St. Louis, phone serviceperson from Phoenix, or babysitter in Sioux City. When it comes to the opportunity to do more, a Montana ranch hand is on equal footing with a Madison Avenue executive. Most mothers can outdo professors of productivity at major universities . . . And YOU—no matter what your age, sex, location, education, size, race, or creed may be—have the same advantages and disadvantages when it comes to time use that people with big names and titles have. The clock runs the same for all of us—plain old everyday people or rich, powerful, and famous ones. You have the knowledge and desire, and hear the same whispering of the spirit that **you can do more and better**—so now get rid of the "time scholar stigma," the idea that high producers are some kind of extraordinary person that you can never hope to be.

I meet thousands of people who, because they don't have a lot of formal education, think they're unqualified to be masters of doing more. And I meet thousands of others who, because they have attended some of the best schools and universities, think they have the inside track. Both types are wrong, as far as time use and production are concerned. Stop worrying about a lack of formal learning, or those letters you have after your name. The only abbreviations that really count here are A.M. and P.M.

We are all ordinary. And you know as well as I do that any of us has the capacity to do more in life than we are doing right now. I've worked and mixed with all kinds of people, from the farms of the West to the fancy studios of the world's largest TV networks and the offices of some of this country's biggest organizations and companies. I've taught in schools, run many businesses, hired tens of thousands of people, authored many books, entertained and spoken to hundreds of thousands of people in the course of more than 10,000 public appearances.

And I know from repeated experience that a little "extra" is all it takes to make a person extraordinary.

Extra is easy to understand and within the reach of all of us—you, me, anyone who wants it. So just add *extra* to *ordinary* and there—YOU are one of those *extraordinary* people you hold in awe!

What Is the Secret?

You'll find the answer to this question by figuring out what common virtue all of the following people have. They're not all physically attractive or rich, not the same race or religion, and some are educated while some are not. Their similarity is a simple one . . .

> **A retired farmer,** sixty-five years old, was hired by a contractor to do odd jobs and construction projects. He worked with three other employees—strong, young college-age men all doing the same kind of work. In a couple of months, the old man was the **only employee,** and he did all the work and did it better and faster than his three former colleagues put together.

A young lieutenant colonel retired from the Air Force, and along with many of his high-ranking comrades, faced a bleak employment situation in civilian life. While his friends looked for the best-paying jobs they could possibly find, refusing most because of their "overqualification," this fellow took a $24,000-a-year job, with bonuses for bonus results. By his second year, he was making $200,000.

A twenty-five-year-old wrestling teacher launched his own painting business (he'd never painted in his life). He made money, friends, and customers. Then he decided to become a house builder, right at the worst possible time (high interest rates, right in the middle of a recession, etc.). He'd never built a thing in his life, but he moved to a likely area and started right in, with no backing or well established background. In just one year, during which many of the old experienced builders "went under," this young developer had $50,000 in profits in his pocket, had twenty-two new houses under way, and was designing and building his own dream house, too. He did plenty of free, donated work for his church and community as well.

Most of the local farmers took care of less than 200 acres of row crops, with the aid of a small army of helpers. A man moved into the area and cultivated and cared for 400 acres of row crops, with no hired help, just family. He made a big profit and had time to enjoy himself, too.

A resort operated the same way for thirty-eight years, with the same number of people to do the maintenance. It took forty-five people in all. A young man cleaning phone booths near the resort stopped in and talked himself into an opportunity to contract the work. Eventually, he was able to replace the forty-five people with fifteen and the quality of the work only improved.

A high-intensity office of corporate executives needed top efficiency out of the office assistant. So they pooled their work and a mature, adept, well educated, and experienced woman would arrive early and slave away. She poured out the paperwork and drafts in total dedication. Then a part-time substitute, a shy farm girl with only a high-school education, assumed the job and accomplished more (and more accurately) in two hours than her predecessor did in eight.

A young woman who worked in a copy center for minimum wage was admired for her hustle and accuracy by a customer and then hired by that customer to work for his company. Within two years, she handled all the marketing, copywriting, layout, printing, mailings, scheduling, media contacts, training of others in the office on the computer, payables, and receivables, and she took care of every errand around. Her accuracy and hustle only expanded with the "more."

There are hundreds more stories like this, of situations wherein time was used better somehow, some way, by people—just common, ordinary folks—who managed to do more. There is no big secret here; it's just everyday people applying some simple ideas and principles, and adding that little extra that can make any of us extraordinary.

The retired farmer came in at 7:30 A.M. and got his tools ready, and by 8:00 he was working. He didn't run, just plodded along. But he didn't take long lunches, he never stopped working to talk, he never took breaks, and he never had to fix anything twice. He loved every minute of his work and a long list of people wanted to hire him.

The young lieutenant colonel made 200 calls per day to his clients. He was at the office at 7:00 A.M. and he treated his customers like gold. His colleagues made forty calls/contacts a day, got to work at 8:30, and, once they gained an account, they forgot about the customer.

The twenty-five-year-old teacher studied building two hours a day, in the late nights or early mornings, while he was still teaching. He never used prime work time to visit or daydream.

The man who moved to the farm planned carefully, and plowed even when it was cold. He spent less than he took in and stayed home and worked more than he roamed the town.

The new contractor at the resort didn't have a chance to learn all of the ways to avoid work and kill time while still getting paid. He simply had his people work all the time they were on the job, and thus they got the job done a lot faster as well as better.

The shy Wyoming farm girl had nine brothers and sisters, and knew from earliest childhood not only how to shoulder a full load, but how to cheerfully help with and assume chores besides her own. She carried this habit of output with her to the office, and the work was a piece of cake for her.

The corporate superwoman who went from a copier's minimum wage to maximum output has a special accomplisher's attitude: "I'm at my best when overrun with work, job demands, and opportunities." The only word she ever misspells is *work*—she spells it f-u-n.

Yes, You Can Do More

We hear "I can't find the time . . ." or, "As soon as I find some time I'll . . ." again and again as an excuse to be static. Time doesn't need to be found, it's in plain sight, loudly ticking away. How we use time is the real question.

Consider a college student who takes on a class schedule of the average four-year course of study. Most students think they are suffering and sacrificing to get through this, and when carrying a "full load" figure they are about "maxed out." During my years in college and in the years since, I've a chance to observe students of all ages, eighteen to sixty. Some are completely busy just attending classes and cashing checks from grants, scholarships, and their folks. Others attend classes, work full time, have families, and take part in extracurricular activities. Others do even more than that! My partner Arlo, as a full-time pharmacy student with four children, worked on a job ten hours a day and did lots of church and community work, too. And he was better ranked when he graduated than his fellow students, who (often supported by others) just went to class and studied all the time.

When my wife and I enrolled in school, we were married and totally self-supporting. In the next five years, while a full-time student, I started a cleaning business and built it up to a big company that employed hundreds of other students. We earned our degrees and had four children during our college years. We bought a house, and were active in church, community work, and student government. I was also on the debate team, and played and lettered three years as a college athlete. We took the kids all over, sang in choirs, even pursued hobbies, all while full-time students—and we still had time and could have done more. Looking back now, we view that as a pretty simple, easy time.

Sure, one class, course, or commitment can keep you busy and use up all your time, if that's what you want and expect and accept out of yourself. But you can do more, lots more. **You are a human being, capable of all kinds of incredible accomplishments and creations.** Surely using time better and stacking in a few more blocks to build a better life isn't asking too much.

The biggest inhibitor of "more" is waiting for an outside force to do it for us, to drag us up by the bootstraps—the company, the government, or our parents. Some don't doubt that they can and should do more, but they feel they need someone or something to step into their lives and lift them up to the effort. As for the "at my age" cop-out, what difference does age make? No one is too young or too old to do more. For some reason, we've gotten in the habit of not expecting much out of the young or the old. Well, why not? Those are some prime times of life! Young, we have energy, strength, ambition, unequaled imagination, and time. Old, we have wisdom and experience. Why do we move our mature people to the Never Never Land called retirement? That's a lot of smarts wasted. Who said you're supposed to wind down with the years?

I've known people who, under terrible pressure and in impoverished conditions, have cared for disadvantaged children in the midst of forty other jobs and responsibilities, and it only strengthened them. Seldom is there truly "too much" to do; most people just have other unsolved or unresolved things nagging at them, so they never dedicate their time and energy to the work.

Years ago, when I was living in the Sun Valley resort area, I was called to preside over a church congregation with the authority to appoint others in the congregation to help with the teaching, singing, services, visiting the sick, helping the needy, and other jobs. The congregation was small at first, but we still needed a full staff to run the different programs. Most of the volunteers were doing four separate church jobs, such as teaching a class on Sunday, another during the week, counseling youth, and helping with church welfare efforts. Those were fun and progressive days, everyone had a lot to do and did it well. They were cheerful and committed; they were needed and they knew it. They wouldn't and really couldn't miss church or one of their assignments.

As the area grew, more and more people moved in, and soon each member only had three jobs. They didn't seem to have quite the same fire in them, or as much time for church affairs. More people joined, and then each member only had two jobs. The volunteers still did okay, but they weren't nearly as go-getting as they'd been when they had four. Once the congregation was big enough so that each volunteer only had one assignment, some of the real performers with four jobs before were real draggers. They simply didn't enjoy their one task as much they had enjoyed four. And all the complaints now were about time shortage!

We see this in all types of jobs, all types of athletic teams, in the Army, and in the classroom. When the demands are hard, more than normal—straining, even—people will respond and be activated and inspired to do more and better than they do on a lighter schedule.

My company once cleaned buildings at 1,500 square feet an hour. That was shining, unbeatable, maximum time use—we thought. Then we came up against the tougher big-city competition and learned to clean at 2,500 square feet an hour—beyond belief! Today, we are bidding and cleaning those same buildings at 5,000 to 6,000 square feet an hour! Amazing what necessity (we *need* to keep making money) enables one to do.

A field supervisor in the pineapple fields of Hawaii told me a similar story one afternoon. "For twenty years, workers in the fields here were planting 5,000 and 6,000 plants per day; that was what was expected and that was what was done. If someone managed 7,000, it was awesome. One day a young man from Idaho, not knowing how many to plant per day, did 12,000. Now most are doing far more."

Most of us consciously or unconsciously do what is *average*, what's been done and accepted before. If one report a day is par, then one report is done. Then as someone is busy doing that one daily report, a new manager walks in and says "I always get two reports a day out of my people, and that's how it will be if you want to be one of my people." The manager gets two reports a day, and none of the workers can understand what happened; they don't *feel* any busier even though they are accomplishing more.

While doing a study once for a telephone company in Chicago, I noticed that one of their top cleaners only cleaned two restrooms a day. But boy, were they clean. You almost had to shield your eyes when you walked into them. And so this fellow and his boss received constant praise. The boss, who had never gotten compliments for restrooms before, thought all was well and didn't want to rock the boat. But any janitor can clean 500 square feet of restroom per hour. I informed the boss that the person doing the great job on the two could easily, without any strain at all, do seventeen more in the day just as clean. So the boss assigned nineteen and that fellow is now is doing nineteen daily and they look just as good as those original two.

Johnny Weissmuller, the original movie Tarzan, held many a world swimming record in his day. For years those records were unthreatened—no one could imagine being as good as Tarzan. Today, thirteen- and fourteen-year-old boys and girls are swimming faster at better times than old Tarzan could have imagined.

Can you (ordinary you) do better? Can you do more? You sure can. The producers you admire do it, and most of them are not as talented, well educated, or young as you are. There's nothing wrong with you. Maybe you've just never seriously considered doing more or realized the rewards for it. It's easy for us to get into a rut or a set way of doing things, and never realize anything is wrong until a competitor drastically outperforms us and takes our position, spirit, and sometimes even our relationships away from us.

Accomplishment, the Great Motivator

Dreams, promises, stories, and projections of success are nothing compared to a taste of success! Getting ready to do can generate some enthusiasm, but nothing turns us on like "finished." "I did it." "Done!" "Mission accomplished." Once you've moved a mountain, or even a molehill or two, you'll find yourself clicking your heels and ready to start on the next one. For a doer, one accomplishment just provides the fuel for more! Yes, you can do more, and once you get started, you'll never want to stop.

What's the Catch?

It seems that whenever we have a real conviction and determination to upgrade or change ourselves, some shadow of doubt slows us down or backs us off. Right now, you're cautiously asking, "What am I going to have to DO (buy, learn) to accomplish more?" Relax—nothing hard, strange, or expensive. In fact, as you'll see in the next chapter, to do more you start by doing less!

Take this Productivity Test to determine what kind of a producer you are. Check any boxes that apply to you. Add up the checkmarks and score yourself in each column.

Productivity Test of Traits

Low Producer	High Producer
❑ Generally late	❑ Always early
❑ Looks for less to do	❑ Looks for more to do
❑ Lays low when wounded	❑ Works while wounded
❑ Avoids hard work	❑ Enjoys hard work
❑ Plays a lot	❑ Plays enough
❑ Watches the clock	❑ Races the clock
❑ Lives in the past	❑ Learns from the past
❑ Often out of control	❑ In control of self
❑ Sleeps excessively	❑ Sleeps as needed
❑ Maximum amount of TV	❑ Minimum amount of TV
❑ Passive	❑ Active
❑ Makes excuses	❑ Makes it happen
❑ Lives by tradition	❑ Sets new precedents
❑ Must be asked	❑ Takes the initiative
❑ Easily distracted	❑ Hard to distract
❑ Follower	❑ Thinker/leader
❑ Whines about injustices	❑ Accepts injustices
❑ Waits	❑ Goes ahead without if
❑ Plays it safe	necessary
❑ Walks	❑ Takes risks
	❑ Runs
_____ Total Boxes Checked	_____ Total Boxes Checked

Scoring

13–20: Read this book twice and put it into practice!

11–16: Not quite good enough! Read the rest of the book and you'll be sure to do better.

9–15: Average . . . that doesn't really cut it in the world of high producers.

4–9: Be proud of yourself! (And keep it up!)

1–3: You're awesome—nobody's that good!

Scoring

18–20: You're awesome— nobody's that good!

13–17: Be proud of yourself! (And keep it up!)

11–16: Average . . . that doesn't really cut it in the world of high producers.

9–15: Not quite good enough! Read the rest of the book and you'll be sure to do better.

1–9: Read this book twice and put it into practice!

Chapter 3
A Little Subtraction . . .
Adds a Lot of Production

One afternoon in the "old corral" back on the ranch, I was out in the middle of the herd doing my utmost to catch one of the steers to check its eye infection. Even with just one good eye, the steer was successfully eluding me. It would run around, through, and behind the fifty other cows in the corral. The other cows (who thought I was after them, too) were racing around everywhere, with tails arched and hooves flying. They would shield the infected steer, jump in front just as I was tossing the rope, and get in my way when I was trying to run him down, totally frustrating my efforts. My dad watched me chase and toss until my throat was dry from manure dust, then said, "If you'd get some or all of those other cows out of there, you'd handle the one easier." I did just that, and finally caught my critter on the first toss.

How often do we find ourselves trying to focus on a task or goal, while scores (even hundreds) of other things are milling around it, leaping and crowding and hanging and bouncing in our way—creating confusion and eating up time? These other "cows" are not necessarily bad, nor do they need to be banished forever, but they sure need to be out of the way so you can get on with the program at hand. Here is a case where subtraction will usually mean some real additions.

You are going to love this part of getting more time to use, because I'm not going to load you down with a thick planner notebook or an elaborate filing system. No, I won't recommend any programs, classes, or courses, nor will I teach you any theories, formulas, or clever maneuvers. I'm not going to ask you to drill yourself in anything, only to **discard**!

That means shed, toss, ditch, and dump whatever is holding you back. You already have "the time"—all you have to do is uncover it and use it.

I know you want some specifics now, so let's look at some of the things suffocating your forty-eight-hour clock. Some of these are actually good and worthwhile; it's when they exist **in excess** that they become a problem.

Junk and Clutter

The very first step to becoming a high producer is to stop accumulating and start eliminating. In other words, **dejunk**!

Get rid of not only that junk in your attics, garages, and closets (and all the other useless things we spend so much time buying, storing, shuffling, and sorting) but also the less tangible things like habits and associates that waste time.

It doesn't take any advanced degrees to figure out that it takes time to tend to excess—the frills, the extras, all the physical and mental clutter we carry around. It's so logical, yet so seldom done. We usually don't toss the trivial till we're forced to, or until we get serious about excelling and reaching our peak performance.

Some competitive swimmers shave their heads, legs, chests, armpits—anything that has hair on it. This is because hair and even a button or emblem on a swimsuit can slow you down.

Trimming the trivia and trashing it is fun, costs nothing, and has guaranteed results—**more available time**.

Get Rid of Those Excess Objects

At even the very busiest times in my life, I've found I could almost double my output by dejunking.

Junk and clutter in and around our homes, lives, and workstations account for an amazing amount of wasted time and emotion. There are probably more arguments, family fights, divorces, and business failures as a result of junk than anything else except finances. Have you ever stopped to add up the amount of *life* and *time* consumed by ownership of things?

Keeping things neat and uncluttered is one of the best ways to insure speed and efficiency. We can't do much go-getting if we have to constantly dig and hunt for what we need, and dodge and squeeze around things. Keeping no-account stuff around, or things that are no longer needed, is like keeping the scaffolding up after the building is built or painted. It looks bad and just gets in the way.

If you've done the job, you don't need to leave scraps and trimmings and leftovers around to prove that you did it, or how—the fact that the new structure stands is evidence enough. And if there's a lot of even high-class junk around, we spend a lot of time fiddling with it and polishing and protecting it. And the more we have, the more we accumulate.

Get rid of anything you don't use or want. Don't love what can't love you back. **Top producers are seldom junkers.**

Prune Before You Prioritize!

There's a lot going on these days—even a sedate life in the early twenty-first century is about three times as active as a barnstorming life in the early twentieth. We're not just bombarded, we're saturated with information, events, offers, and opportunities. If we just go stand somewhere, we can have more happen to us in ten minutes than in ten days of earlier times.

Sorting and processing all the new possibilities and problems dumped on us daily can, will, and does consume a lot of time. This isn't productivity, though—it's just activity. You can easily end up old, tired, and troubled, without having been anywhere or accomplished anything. How many times have you heard or said to yourself, "I've been running all day, I'm dead tired, and I haven't really gotten anywhere"?

In an effort to deal with all this, most people attempt to follow the great production principle known as "prioritizing." Simply putting all the activities you think you need to do in order of importance will get you nowhere except further buried and stressed out. First, before you do anything else, ignore or weed out the unnecessary (you know what it is) and you won't have to labor over most of those great management words like delegate and prioritize.

Don't sit there trying to prioritize 10,000 "things to do"— it uses up time and confuses you. It's far more important to identify the truly necessary out of the incredible number of things available to us each day. The first move of a real getter-doner is to get rid of activities and options you don't really want or need, things that are just muddying the water. It's a lot easier to prioritize 1,200 things a year than 10,000, and a lot more of them are likely to actually get done.

Eliminate That Excess Baggage

Even good stuff can bog you down if you have too much of it. Carrying too much with you everywhere ends up hurting the goal rather than helping. It's easy to spend so much time gathering equipment and help that we never get to the job. All of the people and parts you might need for a task do have to be roomed and boarded, transported and tended.

Over the years, the more I've condensed my tools, vehicles, library, wardrobe, travel kit, and suitcase contents, the more I get done. At first, when I moved from task to task, I had to have a pickup to haul all my stuff in. As I gradually reduced the size of my arsenal, eliminated duplication in my equipment, and shook things down to the essentials, I found I could still manage to do the job—and now I didn't have to manage a bunch of things as well. I used to carry a big axe and a little hatchet in my tool box; now I have one middle-sized axe, which means one thing less to lose and look for, or blame someone else for carrying off after I've left it lying around.

Noises and Distractions

Observing a noticeably unproductive part-time clerk attempting to fill inventory in my cleaning supplies store, I asked him about the radio blasting beside him and the TV in the background (he was trying to catch the news while he was at it, too). "How can you pay attention to what you're doing?" I said.

"I need the noise to concentrate," he said.

Lights buzzing, machines whirring, music or TVs blaring, nonstop traffic noise, clearly audible nearby conversations. . . . People may say they can tune out things like this (and maybe some can), but one way or another it feeds into your system. It chips away at and competes with your concentration.

Some kinds of soft music or white noise have been claimed to speed up output, but plain old observation of results will tell you that good producers do not need lots of noise.

The mind has to absorb and process all input, and distractions of any kind always take a toll. Even if you're disciplined on the job, distractions blot out a lot of inspiration and use up energy. I used to say that something might distract me, but it would never divert me. But now I know that continued distraction is bound to end up diversion. Like a pesky fly—first it's only a little distracting, then more and more, and finally the urge to end the buzzing and the challenge of swatting the filthy thing totally occupies you.

High producers are aware of and stay away from their distraction weaknesses. Noise and other distractions drown out too much good working time.

Interruptions

Control interruptions when you have to accomplish something! Easier said than done, right? We do have some crowded days and weeks when eliminating interruptions seems not just impractical, but close to impossible. However, that's not all the time.

It's amazing how much we can get done once we're away from the clamor and chaos. The older and wiser I get, the less time I spend in that assemblage of interruptions known as "the office." There've been times I got to the office first thing in the morning and did nothing but shuffle things, say hello to visitors, paw through junk mail, and chitchat for the first couple of hours—I was never able to start or finish anything. I finally had to get in the car and drive over to the park a couple of blocks away to do my day's work—uninterrupted—in one hour!

Interruptions sidetrack progress and alter our mood. And telephones, as you know, have no mercy. With constant interruption, a half-day's work can easily take three days.

> When we're interrupted, we have to reorganize and start, reorganize and start, reorganize and start—a lot harder than organizing once and **doing**.

How Much Time Are You Losing to Interruption?

Imagine beginning a project, only to have to stop and get up for a tool or a part, over and over again. You'd spend half your day working and half interrupting your work. Random interruptions from outside sources have the same effect. You can easily spend a whole day taking care of interruptions, rather than working. If you're not convinced yet, try this little exercise.

1. When you get up in the morning, list the things you intend to do that day as 1, 2, 3, 4, etc., at the top of a piece of paper.

2. Make another numbered list called "Interruptions" on the bottom half of the sheet, leaving blank spaces after the numbers.

3. Get to work, and note the time you spend on each project, down to the minute.

4. Each time you're interrupted, mark the reason and how much time it took in the appropriate space.

Follow these instructions all day for two or three days. If you need any further convincing, at the end of this trial period figure up the total time lost in interruptions. Then compute how many of your planned accomplishments you could have completed in that time.

Control Your Visitors!

Keep yourself crowded with work, but not with people. A great doer summed up her advice for a lifetime of success: "You can't be 100 percent social and get a lot done." We live to interact with and love people, but too many too often will leave us unable to accomplish much.

Visitors are fun and socializing is fun; they are some of the main ingredients in living a satisfying life. But you need to be able to shut down the switch on this when you have to get things done.

The bottom line is that you cannot accept all invitations, attend all gatherings, take in all events, or stop to talk or chat whenever anyone wants to. This is not because any of this is bad or worthless, but because so much of it just isn't in the direct line of what you need to do. It will also lead you off into other directions, away from your goals.

Remember, you are the master of your own time, not a helpless victim. You are the only one who can control your interrupters. "I wish they'd leave me alone" is a spineless plea. You have to take things into your hands, and here are seven things you can do:

1. Make your operation patterns—your free and busy times— known to everyone. And train them to visit during the free, not the busy, periods.

2. Let out word that you "hate interruptions." (This works wonders, and by itself may eliminate at least 50 percent of the problem.)

3. Demand the courtesy of appointments, or at least advance warning. This makes it easier to stay productive and on track.

4. Be busy. When someone comes unexpectedly, always act busy, as if you are in the middle of something (which you should be, anyway!). Then, you can either offer to stop or keep at it. Ninety-five percent of visitors will take the hint. The remaining five percent are too oblivious to take offense anyway. This helps people get the message, and if they assume that you're "always busy" they'll make ten-minute calls, not the usual two hours. Being honestly busy limits and can eliminate unimportant interruptions.

5. Redecorate to discourage dawdling. A chair by your desk only invites people to visit and stay.

6. Become the aggressor and initiator to end an interruption. Develop some stock phrases that suit you and use them. Learn to say things like "Well, thank you for coming," as a hint that you're moving on to something else. If that doesn't work, don't hem and haw or beat around the bush. Come right out with it. Say, "Gee, it's too bad you happened to come right when I was in the middle of this project. Could we talk/get together another time?" Then you can arrange the stacking of bricks to get more done.

7. If all else fails, put visitors to use. Solicit their help and hand them a hardhat, dishtowel, pen, or whatever.

Find whatever works for you, but do it. Welcome people who are scheduled, as well as those you really want to see. For those who pop in and interrupt, give an abbreviated welcome and excuse yourself and get your work done, "Excuse me, but I have to have this package off to Fed Ex before noon. I sure hope you've enjoyed your visit to these parts."

Run-on Reporting

It is good to keep track of things, but even tracking can go too far. You can get so caught up in charting and chronicling the course that you never reach the destination. You may find yourself focusing on and rewarding reports instead of results.

When we get too busy telling what we can do, we often don't have the time and energy left to do it. Some people get so enthusiastic about tracking and reporting and categorizing events that they forget that **the event**, not the report, is the subject.

Necessary as they are, records are passive, a prediction or a history of production—not production itself! Keeping track is good support for any tracks made, but making those tracks is the target, not measuring and calculating the score.

Finance Fighting

Constant worry about finances—balancing, floating, borrowing, and all the other little activities involved in juggling money—is ultra time- and energy-consuming (if not all-consuming). Life is hard when you're forever fighting finances.

Early in my career, while expanding my business and having to meet large payrolls, I was spending three hours every day just begging for collectibles, hunting up, transferring, and taking care of money. Half of my waking thoughts and dreams were about finances, too. If I had been using all that time for more constructive and progressive activities, I'd probably own three banks by now. Stretching is great for physical fitness, and about the worst thing going for financial fitness! Have you ever added up the time and money spent trying to scrounge up money?

Most of us assume we are cash-short in business or our personal lives for reasons beyond our control, but few financial circumstances are beyond our control. Who can you actually blame it on? Generally it comes back to us—*our* excesses and *our* lack of discipline. The day I decided to quit spending cash I didn't have, quit cussing the bankers and collectors for my problems, and started operating money ahead instead of money behind (on credit), I gained more time than I could believe.

You can alleviate your financial burdens if you ease off and up a little. Force yourself to keep a cash reserve; quit spending to the end and hoping for a windfall. Keep your hands off the working money. Fighting finance (at home or in business)—talking and arguing about it, covering bases, squeaking by, explaining, and accounting for things—is more draining than double the amount of physical toil. Fighting finances is probably one of your biggest nonproductive pastimes right now. It can be changed quite simply. **When you quit the cash hassle your personal productivity will increase tremendously!**

Unhealthy Habits

Your lifestyle, of course, is your own business. There are, however, some inescapable laws of production and go-getting. It's hard to produce without strength and endurance—the best tools, brain, and organizational plan in the world aren't going to make a low-energy person into a high producer. Doing more means putting more sweat and muscle into things, and even if your work is mental, physical vigor makes a difference.

If your health isn't as good as it ought to be, improving it would be one of the first moves to make in becoming a real go-getter When we feel bad we not only suffer discomfort, we're cheated out of the blessings and rewards of doing a lot.

If you have a physical problem you can't change, it may put limits on what you can do, but even then you usually have options for overcoming these limits. The other 90 percent of us with no legitimate physical disability are probably just overweight and under-exercised, and we absolutely can do something to increase strength and capability.

I had a friend who spent many of his evenings playing cards for three to five hours, downing pizza, pretzels, and beer. This, of course, put the weight on and so for two hours the next afternoon he would punish himself brutally, running in sweats with weights. But he wasn't losing any weight. He may have enjoyed his nighttime activities, but he was paying a big price for them. He had no time to be a go-getter, which he desperately wanted to be.

Poor eating and drinking (and any drug) habits zap the life out of you—often permanently. It's hard to be top banana when you feel like a waddling pear.

Society has sold us on the idea that "having fun"—partying all night, feasting on huge greasy dinners, and sitting around in a boat or theater or on a beach—is going to help us live longer and better. Compared to this, work is about the best therapy and menu going!

If you haven't quite had the gumption to lose weight or quit some habits you know aren't doing a thing for you, harness yourself up to a serious workload. This alone will finally force you to start heading toward robust health. Having a commitment to do a lot actually helps keep you well; it's amazing what physical and mental strength you get from doing and accomplishing. For many of our ailments, work—good hard work—is the best cure. And when your work is rewarding, snacks and other sideline things won't interest you all that much!

Correctable Health Problems

None of us is completely innocent of this one: chewing on one side of our mouth or dodging certain foodstuffs because we won't go to the dentist, or limping around and spending several days down or "out" because it's inconvenient or costly to have that foot fixed. Or because we just want to keep on putting it off.

The consequences of genuine health needs and problems are inevitable and delay will only accelerate the cost and pain. They also keep you unfocused, concentrating on the pain you're enduring or the pull to come. Or worrying endlessly about what might be wrong, instead of finding out. All of which takes up or dilutes a major portion of "your time."

If lack of funds for the "fix" in question is the issue, and health insurance is lacking or inadequate, there may be more options than you have considered. Many universities have clinics where dental work can be done for modest fees. Health care providers often have staggered fee schedules and you may qualify for reduced rates. Even hospitals may agree to let you pay for a procedure in monthly installments over time.

And often if you review your spending plans for the next year or two, you will see money that could be much better spent on medical or dental procedures that would make you feel whole and sound again.

Overdone Social Events

People are always getting together to party and "kill" time (like every evening after work). A lifetime can easily go by that way. Fun is fun and getting together can be a real highlight of living and loving, but focusing on partying isn't going to get you far. Life isn't a party, and showing up and standing around at every social event in the world isn't going to do much for accomplishment.

At every convention or trade show I'm hired to speak or perform at, for instance, there is always a cocktail party. People hang on each other's arms, often in a cloud of cigarette smoke, gripping an iced glass of something as if their lives depended on it. Conversations are full of loud laughter, back-patting, and snide remarks. People can be at their worst at a cocktail party, and parties and social events put us all in an easy, non-focused frame of mind. And so most of the "I'll calls," "Please sends," and "How are things goings" end up forgotten and are a complete waste of time as far as getting the job done is concerned. Even as a place to meet people, situations like this are rather diluted for proper bonding.

People will tell you that parties are necessary for getting acquainted, making contacts, advancing causes, and being promoted. But if you show up on the real scene—the work scene—fresh and prepared the next morning, guess who they will all remember the best and even envy.

Food-Centered Living

If eating is the central focus in your life, the thing you plan everything around, and you intend to keep it that way, don't count on becoming a great getter-doner. One of my contracting companies, for example, once had 112 painters literally standing around waiting for the scaffolding to arrive for a big church painting job. When it finally was delivered (by one of my managers), he was forty-five minutes late. His excuse: "Well, I hadn't had lunch, so I stopped down the road to eat."

He didn't have a clue that a skipped, later, or quick meal once in a while means a day or a weekend (or over a lifetime, five or six years, at least) gained to get things done, and to nourish the soul and other people.

My mother-in-law was religious about scheduling things, especially meals. When it's time to eat, everything else stops—

no buts about it. One afternoon, a high wind came up and blew some trash out of my burning barrel. The trash fire spread to the hillside near our house. The fire only had to burn about 200 feet across our yard to reach the brush, and once it did that, it would burn up everything from our ranch to the city, which was about twenty miles of dry brush away.

It was a desperate situation, and I was alone. I grabbed buckets and shovels and went to work on the flames, nearly killing myself just keeping even. The smoke and heat from both the fire and the 100-degree weather were so bad I could scarcely breathe or swallow. The hair on my arms and my eyebrows was singed, and my pant legs kept catching fire, but I couldn't stop. When I was right on the verge of getting slightly ahead of the fire line, saving 80,000 acres of pasture grass and trees and a city, my mother-in-law strolled up to the edge of the fire and hollered in a shrill voice, "It's time to eat—now—come right now. You've got to learn to take care of yourself!" The whole countryside was about to go up in smoke and she wanted to interrupt me for something as incidental as eating.

When you find yourself moving so fast, accomplishing so much that you have to ask, "Did I eat today?" you are getting nearer to the refined fire of self-discipline. **Eating well and regularly doesn't have to mean centering life on food, as so many people do.** Don't let eating ceremonies stand in the way of accomplishment. On an ordinary workday, making eating into an elaborate ritual instead of a refueling process is nonproductive. Some people spend three to four hours per day just *eating*. You can still enjoy your food and family associations at meals if you cut that down to one hour a day.

Some business lunches or dinners do get things done that might never be accomplished in the cut-and-dried setting and ambiance of an office. But there is a point of diminishing returns here.

When I first started to do a lot of traveling, my productivity seemed to fall. I wasn't getting as much done as I once did. Why? In every town I went to, twenty people from the publisher, network, station, or other sponsor were determined to dine their special guest on the expense account, and they'd all pick the nicest and most ceremonial restaurant in town. As a courtesy, and sometimes because I was hungry, I would go. So each night in a different town meant new people and new places, great food, great company. Some of those meals, however, were taking three hours or even more from the time we left the hotel until we returned. Little business was accomplished; it was noisy; and the food was overpriced and overspiced. I suddenly realized I was losing up to thirty hours a week in the new travel world just eating!

Now, even if I'm by myself in the middle of nowhere, I seldom eat out and I get a lot more done. I'm in better health, and it doesn't really offend anyone not to have to spend hundreds of dollars for a meal. I don't have to be irritated by overdone "amenities" anymore, or smokers and noises, lines and crowds. And I give my tip money to charity now and have my thirty hours of time back.

Shopping

Shopping is one of the most unproductive pastimes around. Buying what you need when you need it is a necessary and important part of life, but "shopping" isn't. The majority of people who go shopping (that means wandering aimlessly through the shops and malls, taking in all the latest offerings) are low producers. Shopping extends buying into a social event that uses up tons of time, and ultimately weakens and confuses you into buying things you don't really want or need and can't afford. High producers buy, but seldom shop. But they miss bargains, you say? A quick overpaying for something may beat a drawn-out and labor-intensive underpaying for it. Think about it.

Image Pursuits

Trying to be seen as the Duke and Duchess of your community is a real time-stealer. Getting hung up on the image and status of your home and car, and trying to elevate yourself socially are wastes of time. Who really cares? Those who don't have what you have will just dislike you for having more and showing off. Those on the same level with you won't like you, either, for trying to be as good as them. And those above you, like the neighbor with a Hummer, two gazebos, and an Olympic-size indoor pool, will consider you unnecessarily pretentious.

Having a bunch of glitzy belongings gets you nowhere. It just enriches the junk merchants and the insurance companies. All this takes time and resources to tend.

Best-Dressed Stress

Wonder how many years of our lives clothes take? Just think of all the time spent picking out clothes, putting them on, changing and adjusting them—all that strutting in front of others and the mirror. Fast movers want quick clothes. One time, for instance, my wife offered to pack my shirts and asked me which ones I wanted. "The productive ones," I answered. She came out of the closet with a perplexed look: "Just what is a productive shirt, may I ask?"

"The ones without the two extra buttons on each sleeve and the button-down collar." It takes three times as long to put on and do up a shirt like this. I'm not into clip-on ties for speed yet (I've been tying ties for so long I can do it in seconds), but in general the less lacing and buttoning, belting, snapping, matching, and tucking to do before getting going, the better I like it.

Same goes for jewelry. It takes time to pick it out, and put it on, and take it off—not to mention guard it, and look for it after you set it down somewhere, or drop it down the drain.

Fancy or overly daring clothes cut productivity on the job, too. We can't run, bend, climb, or even breathe deeply because our outfit won't permit it, or we're so preoccupied with how we look that what we're supposed to be doing is lost in the shuffle.

"Dressing for the express lane" might sound a little radical, but it sure speeds up a lot of people. As a rule, the heavy dressers and high stylists are the slowest people on two legs—and the biggest time-consumers.

The same is true for the other grooming and gussying preoccupations, from hair care to makeup. You'll never be effective if vanity overrules sanity.

In the office, the classroom, or at home, production is cheaper and more effective than $500 suits, $50-an-ounce perfume and cologne, and all of that. People love deeds and ignore duds!

Rubbish Reading

Reading is automatically considered worthwhile, if not sacred, and there's no shortage of reading material today. There are more than 60,000 new books published every year, thousands of magazines around of every imaginable type, and daily and weekly newspapers all over the place. Reading takes time, lots of it. If the material is good and beneficial, then it's a productive, enjoyable pastime; if it's not, you're squandering time and brain cells.

I'm a writer, but I'll be the first to tell you that much of what's written and peddled in the form of the printed word is not too profound. Most magazines, for example (except for the

more technical ones), tend to present neutral, middle-of-the-road material. They're usually not going to come forth with anything that takes a hard stand and changes your behavior and buying habits—especially if it might offend advertisers. If I wrote an article about the vacuum cleaner banditry going on today (being forced to pay $600 for a unit worth about $99), and if it were a true, helpful, money-saving article, do you think your favorite home magazine would publish it? Never! It would cost them hundreds of thousands of dollars in lost advertising. Likewise, books that couldn't matter less to your life or anyone else's fill the shelves of bookstores and airport and drugstore bookracks.

Relieve yourself of that rubbish reading, and there'll be more time for those things you really want to do.

"Worked Up for Nothing" Stuff

All of the details of the latest celeb lawsuit or a daytime TV star getting kicked out of someone's bed can really erode your might and mind (as well as your agenda) if you take the time to track it . . . and for what?

This really came home to me one day after watching "my team" lose a big game on TV. I really get into a game and take everything personally, and when I turned off the set, I was irritated and exhausted for hours afterward. I noticed that this had happened several times now, and I realized I had to quit watching if I planned to do anything productive afterward. Don't let your adrenaline be drained by things that aren't even real and are not rewarding.

We waste millions of hours a minute around the world on things like this. The latest big storm is about to hit the eastern seaboard, for example. It's going to be the biggest yet and everyone is told to prepare for it. News is in short supply at the time, so the network begins a campaign of speculating about it. What will happen if? And they build on this until they have four days of tension and nonexistent-as-yet problems solved. Four days of nothing but talk and theorizing. Then the storm backs off and nothing happens. Things like this take your time and emotion and give you nothing back.

Worrying about things we have no control over, or that are really none of our business, can use up a lot of time. You can easily spend two full hours a day just digesting, talking and thinking about, and using up emotion on things that have absolutely no worth at all to you or anyone else. This is downright detrimental.

On my way to a speaking engagement one morning, I jotted down a sample of the daily menu of trivia available to us. One paper (people were laboring through all seventy-eight pages of it that Sunday) had an exact count and description of the number of pairs of shoes a celebrity owned, articles glorifying the lives of losers in detail, tons of descriptions of and praises for new stuff we don't need, a literary critic analyzing which side of the raft Huck Finn got in, a summary of urine reports on Olympic athletes, another annual countdown of celebrities' most embarrassing moments, the latest big politician's womanizing adventures, etc., etc., etc. This kind of sawdust can lead your life, or **YOU** can, and the decision you make here will have a lot to do with whether you become a high producer or not. Even a great man or woman could get lost in this sea of stuff that ultimately matters zero in your life. And it will add up to zero in the future, too. You can't spend your time and emotion tending to trivia day after day.

You alone can make the value judgment here—you know what's really contributing to your life and goals and what isn't. If you can't do anything about it, or it doesn't affect the outcome of your life or that of others you care about, then don't waste time arguing or worrying about it, or betting on it. You'll gain a lot of time from dejunking this stuff and have time to make news instead of reading it.

Tears Over Spilled Milk

I broke a window once and was pretty despondent over it—"Don't cry over spilled milk," my mother said. At the age of eight, I couldn't see much of a relationship between milk and windows, but I sure do now. One of the poorest ways to use time—in fact, the most useless—is "stew time." When something is over and done with and yields some unalterable result, stewing, moping, fuming, and fretting over that outcome is a totally unrewarding consumption of the hours and minutes of our life.

Working up a lather when there's nothing there to wash is futile, as is keeping yourself on simmer or even boil for a day (or even months and years) after an argument or incident is over and done. This particular form of self-punishment is a popular pastime, even though no one ever admires you for how well and passionately you apply yourself to spending time so stupidly.

Agitation and production are not even in the same vocabulary. Staying in a tizzy over a totally unchangeable thing just throws your production gear into neutral so you burn up all your fuel sitting still (if not moving backward!).

As a contractor who often worked for and genuinely admired the world's best telephone operation, I bawled and argued over the breakup of the Bell System for months, until I finally decided, "Hey, it isn't right but I'm not going to change it. It's going to mean poorer service and higher phone costs for all of us, but it's done and I'm not going to be able to do a thing about it. So I better forget it and earn more to pay the bills."

Don't spend your time and effort dwelling on events or circumstances that can't be stopped, restored, redirected, or resolved. Don't dwell on or mire yourself in emotional turmoil over old injuries or things you can't do anything about. Anguishing over past losses—people or profits—is a 100 percent unproductive activity.

The Gnawers

Gnawer? That means something that's gnawing or nagging at you—generally not a little face-it-in-a-moment thing, but something that's bugging and worrying you constantly, causing stress and anxiety you really don't need.

On the ranch, we called it a burr under the saddle or a pebble in the boot, meaning that you can still ride and still walk, but it'll feel pretty uncomfortable. That feeling is not going to help you get more done! The short stop it takes to unsaddle or remove your boot and dislodge the irritant is always worth the interruption.

If you can feel anything gnawing, then you better de-gnaw. It's like having something in your eye. If it's in there you have to get it out, even the smallest hair or tiniest bit of sand. If you leave it there, it will do damage. There are enough unpreventable ruinations around without setting yourself up for any more.

Guilt and Grudges

Feelings of guilt and grudges are among the worst of the gnawers. A clear conscience is a big key to production.

Confucius (who, admittedly, may not have known he was speaking about personal productivity) said, "There are three marks of a superior man: being virtuous, he is free from anxiety; being wise, he is free from perplexity; being brave, he is free from fear." Each one of those three virtues frees up time. When you analyze what really consumes time and energy, nothing rates higher than anxiety. When you do an evil deed, you have the constant anxiety afterward of worrying about getting caught. You are constantly using up good logic and energy creating rationalizations, just in case you are found out. So if you have done something that's keeping you up nights, apologize, confess, pay up, or whatever—but don't keep carrying it around with you. It's eating away at your time.

Bearing grudges and nursing hard feelings is a real time- and spirit-waster, too—it takes lots of effort to keep score. Replaying in our minds and recounting to others the injustices we've endured, what they said and did and what we said or did in return, is fruitless all around. Uncomplicate things and forget it. If something is bugging you, some hard feelings or a little vendetta in the family or at work, either drop it and get it out of your mind or go to the person to have it out and get it over with.

Likewise, if you're carrying a burden of guilt or backlog of things you failed to do or take care of in the past, either forget them or do whatever you have to do to make them right, right now. You'll get a lot more done and have a lot more fun if you're unencumbered!

||||||||||||||||||||||||||||||||||||||||||||||||||||||||||||||||||||||||||

A duty dodged is like a debt unpaid; it is only deferred, and we must come back and settle the account at last.—J. F. Newton

||||||||||||||||||||||||||||||||||||||||||||||||||||||||||||||||||||||||||

Pettiness

Every single person on this earth packs the capacity for anger, jealousy, revenge, irritation, malice, and many other unfortunate forms of behavior. But the people who yield to these behaviors are seldom producers because they use the clock to count injustices. They spend most of their energy focusing on and overreacting to the everyday human failings of others, instead of helping us all to step beyond to more important matters.

We call this constant brooding over little tiffs and jealousies about position, promotion, someone's new car, etc., pettiness. To a petty person, a minor misstep or oversight is a major melodrama. I've seen people lose three hours of work over losing their place in the cafeteria line, as they complained to everyone about this invasion of their line space by some inconsiderate and obnoxious interloper. That's petty, and it only gets in the way of production. Pettiness charges for its time, too—time and a half!

The Big Five Most Wanted TiME BANDiTS

1. Beverage Rituals

I vote for "beverage rituals" as the most deadly opponent of getting more done. It seems everyone is forever clutching a cup of coffee or a "Giant Gulp" of soda at work, in the car, or anywhere. What a nuisance to have to keep track of—not to mention that it's addictive, unhealthy, unsightly, and a stain and cleanup problem. But worst of all is the amount of time that tending to such things takes out of our lives—it's incredible.

The average coffee drinker consumes more than 70,000 cups of coffee in a lifetime, for example. Even if you don't brew it yourself, that's 70,000 or more times you have to find your cup, fill it, add cream or sugar, carry it to your work station, pick it up, set it down (repeat this at least fourteen or fifteen times), then dump the part that got cold.

The average "coffee break" does little to increase productivity. But it does accomplish the spread of gossip and contempt and criticism of the employer, customers, etc. Breaks can be spent in much healthier and more positive ways. Look around at your next coffee break—few if any of the high producers will be there (and that ought to tell you something).

**You can you use your time to sip,
or to zip through the assignments of life.**

2. Oversleeping

There's no lack of sleep analyzers, and when magazines get hard up for an article someone is always happy to expound on the art of sleeping, or a new theory of sleep needs. There are always revolutionaries who say four hours is enough for anyone, and those who insist eight hours or more plus maybe a nap at noon is the only way to go through life.

Most people have a firm idea of the amount of sleep they need, and this is a very individual matter. But habit and preconception do enter in here. If you want to be more productive, confining your sleeping to just enough time to get a good rest is the answer. The best producers I know are get-up-early-in-the-morning people. I hardly ever see a late sleeper or oversleeper accomplish much. Try cutting even a half-hour off your sleeping, and keep yourself stimulated so you won't need a nap because you're bored, and watch how much more work you get done.

3. Excess Play Time

A lot of people feel they need tons of play to offset work or they'll be out of balance. So we buy boats, scooters, snowmobiles, and other gizmos that cost a lot and make us feel guilty if we don't use them.

Recreation *is* productive and great for a change, as are vacations. But our kids are raised learning more about time-off activities than how to achieve or produce.

Don't get too concerned about the percentage of playtime in your life. The most energetic, dynamic, enthusiastic, positive, and popular people I know play less than average or hardly at all. Most high producers find their play in their work.

Excess playing is unproductive; it gives little back in later years and does nothing to build lives or security. Constant pleasure-seekers just get spoiled and lazy and drizzle their lives away. Relaxation needs a foundation to rest on—one called "industry" or, in plain everyday language, "work." Well-planned play can be therapeutic, educational, and productive . . . if it's counterbalanced with work.

You can do crossword puzzles to develop and enjoy the use of words, or you can write articles or books. You can pedal a stationary bike or go out and make a garden. Why not go for pastimes that have some net worth?

4. Spectating

Sure, we all love to watch a ball game, movie, or race, but continually? We'd end up with nothing except time used up. These things are, after all, just games or performances, not real life. If we spend too much time watching others do all the moving, we'll soon be eliminated from the game.

Spectating is one of the easier unproductive pastimes to fall into. All we have to do is stop for a few minutes, and the spectacle at hand takes over our mind and wits. Sometimes we need a break like this, but big-time watchers are seldom big-time producers!

The average American spends roughly 2,000 hours a year being a spectator or listener. Probably more than half of this time is spent on television. That means the average one of us is spending four hours a day (*twelve years* of our entire life!) watching TV. Impressive, that one activity could occupy so much of our time. Television offers the greatest imaginable variety of ways to waste time. A football game, an informational program, or a movie or two are great and a pleasure to sit in our living room and experience, but four to five hours a day for weeks and months and years on end is more like immobilization and decay.

If you can't seem to get much done lately, switch off the TV, move it out, or drape a quilt over it for month. You'll think you're a resurrected being! Your productivity will make such an upswing that it'll leave you breathless, and you'll even feel better physically.

5. The Computer Coma

We are always on the lookout for tools and resources that will enable us to do things faster and easier, and nothing has emerged yet that equals the computer! It can perform marvels beyond description, but as with most "gems" in life, it comes with some overburden, as veins of gold are surrounded by masses of much less valuable rock. The good products of the computer are often buried in overkill, and sorting through all this sometimes requires as much time as doing things the old way—or even more.

Computers can easily do more than we need done. They offer perfect everything—from games to shopping to editing, sexual stimulation, investments, news, weather, information, and instant non-thought-out communication of all kinds—beyond even what the TV can provide on its best day. We easily end up sidetracked or immersed in trivia that consumes tons of time, all under the illusion that because something is fast and attractive, it is to the point. Or we find ourselves thinking that because we are seated at a desk and using a keyboard, what we are doing on the computer is work.

We can get so enamored of the capacities of our computers that we let them cross the line between give and take, so we find ourselves playing more than producing on them. A much more alarming notice on your computer screen than the word "virus" should be the word "useless"—if it would only flash when we interrupt a productive process to read or review some incidental, inconsequential, nonessential (yet attractive) bit of trivia!

This list could go on for the rest of the book, but you know your own junk and clutter better than anyone. I just want to get you thinking about how easy some simple surrendering of clutter is, in exchange for a chance to get more done. Time to do all those "wants and wishes," all those things that have been waiting, that you've been holding back on.

Notice that I haven't said much about *how* to dejunk these things. I've called your attention to them, confident that you already know how, and I promise that the time you gain will make it worth your while to act.

Real producers have or get the guts to make the cuts when and where they're needed—"lean and mean," they call it. But once you're lean, you don't generally have to be mean, because you have all that extra time.

"But I Just Don't Have the Time . . ."

How often do we find ourselves saying, "I want to, I'd like to, I will . . . as soon as I have the time."

After doing TV appearances with and later reading the reports of some "time analyzers" (who actually studied how and where we use it all), I've become confident that all of us can find a few weeks or days or years to do the things we really want to do. According to these experts, such as Tom Heymann in his book *In an Average Lifetime,* the average American in his or her lifetime spends:

- 1,086 days "sick"
- Three years in meetings
- Thirteen years watching TV
- Eight months opening junk mail
- Seventeen months drinking coffee and soft drinks
- Two years on the telephone
- Five years waiting in line
- Nine months sitting in traffic
- Four years cooking and eating
- A year and a half grooming
- A year and a half dressing
- Seven years in bathrooms
- Three and a half years shopping
- One year looking for misplaced items
- Twenty-four years sleeping

These figures were compiled in 1991, so some of them have changed a bit. But I'd bet my bottom dollar that the new totals would not be any lower, and there are new sources of time waste that now exist and are not even included in this list! Some of these things you could cut by 50 percent and only be better off for it. That will give you back at least ten years of precious time!

That Surprising Spare Time

If you could push a button and have a count of your "off" (wasted, lazy, occupied with nothing) hours for the last year, you'd discover that most of us have at least 1,500 hours of "spare time." What if those could be converted to productive accomplishments and handed to you as a surprise, such as:

1. A check for $8,000
2. Sixteen articles written for major magazines
3. A certificate indicating that you did indeed learn to play the piano
4. Forty thank-you letters from charities, hospital visits
5. Seven good books read
6. Citywide Top Yard and Garden award for the year
7. Coach of the Year for helping three junior teams
8. Two paintings finished, blue ribbon at the fair
9. Two college classes completed (six credit hours)

All of this—or more—you could do with your off, idle, wasted hours. If all of this was yours, do you think you'd be dragging butt at the end of the year? Not a chance! You'd be leaping and strutting like a new colt in high clover.

One afternoon, I ran into a friend who had struggled with a weight problem forever. He'd fought it and fought it and hated every minute of it. He'd been on diets and every milkshake meal ever invented, but to no avail. My friend was trim and happy now. "How?" I asked.

"You know, Don, it was something so simple. I was told to make a list of all I ate. That sounded stupid, but I did it. Every time I ate something, I wrote it down . . . every little morsel. And man, what a surprise when I finished writing. I had a list twelve times as long as the one I kept in my mind. I found out I was eating enough for four people. It didn't seem like it when I was snacking and piecing. Once I saw the numbers, I was awakened to my problem. I'd sure underestimated what I ate!"

How much time we have and waste is surprising, too. Log your time for a week—record all the big and little pieces spent doing what—and you'll see tons of useless activities. A lot of them are things you don't even enjoy, so toss them off and out of your life.

One of my own average days, for example, might analyze out as follows:

Sleeping—6 hours

Grooming—15 minutes

Eating—45 minutes

Interview or other media activity—2 hours

Speaking/Seminars—2 hours

Writing—4 hours

Meetings—30 minutes

Cleaning company business—1 hour

Church—15 minutes

House cleaning/home maintenance—1 hour

WHAT ABOUT THE OTHER 6¼ HOURS? That's the point exactly. I have six-plus hours to do more of what I want and like to do. Once you eliminate time wasters, you'll find you have the same!

Chapter 4

The Mainspring: Direction

We've all tried it, to assemble or make something without a set of directions. The results are usually disgusting, disastrous, or downright ridiculous. Yet the task is clear, all the parts are there, and we've seen others do it. You have all the tools, so why not figure it out as you go along?

I've lain down and bawled after attempting to build or fix something when the directions were not in the box. It usually triples the time involved and you almost always have to backtrack. When you have the directions you do it right, and it's much easier and faster.

Direction without an "s" is just as important. It's the dynamo of doing.

Sometimes athletic teams loaded with talent and desire thrash and fumble until a new coach steps in and outlines a direction. Trace most teenage troublemakers' biggest lack, and you'll find they are lacking direction. Business failure, marriage failure—check it out and you'll find out there was no clear route, rules, or reasoning there. Try to make any human undertaking function well without direction and you are doomed from the start.

Lots of direction comes quietly and naturally from good parents, teachers, and friends, but too many people "make it up as they go along" rather than make any kind of map to chart their course in life.

I guess I've always taken direction for granted. One evening I was having an in-depth conversation with my wife and we were discussing how we might assist several friends who were depressed, stressing out, and unfulfilled. I told my wife that I could see no reason why—these particular people were dripping with talent, education, and ability, in an excellent position to pick their work, location, or associates. "Yes," Barbara said, "but they haven't a clue as to what they want or where they are going." Bingo! They had no direction. They had better sails than others, but they couldn't or wouldn't ever set the sail. They just stuck the sail up in the wind and had been blown all over the ocean of life all their lives. They may have had some thrills, but they didn't reach any ports. On the other hand, I've seen untalented, obnoxious, totally self-centered people do well, and live successful, productive lives, all because they had a direction and stuck to it.

All kinds of great skills, instincts, and abilities are built right into us. Our senses are so marvelous; our capacity to understand, love, and accomplish is awesome. Every human has those, but not necessarily direction. Believe it or not, few people really know where they're going and why, even at the ages of thirty-five or fifty. Life is going on all around them, and they just step out into it, hook up to someone, some cause, or some company, and wait to see where it takes them. They do sometimes choose a place to live, a job, or someone to marry. But at bottom they don't know what they want or what they're after. They're just going to see what happens and react to it as it comes along. "I'll see what comes up" is their theme.

Motion alone doesn't mean much (except that you are alive)—it's where you're moving that matters. You may have heard the old joke, "I don't know where I'm going, but I'm making good time." Well, when you don't know where you're going or why, you can't make good time, plus you won't even know it when you get there!

We've all heard someone say, "Boy, that guy is lucky! He always seems to be in the right place at the right time." It isn't luck—it's direction. That "guy" has chosen a road to travel, a way, and a time. Human imperfection might cause us to sometimes run off the road, pick the middle of the road, or run out of gas on the road, but **once we've decided and chosen a direction, we have a road to follow.**

What do I mean by "direction" here? Direction is the act of making conscious choices about the ethical standards and health rules you want to live by, the education and career you want to pursue, your responsibility to society and your fellow citizens, your relationships with your family and other loved ones in the years ahead. You cannot waffle or wait on this. Many people get stuck at major intersections in life, because they are still trying to make these decisions. If you have direction, you know before you get to the intersection which turn you will take.

Don't wait for a crossroads before attempting to figure out where you are going with your life and projects. Do it now! If you just drift along with what happens to be there or what is available right now—someone else's opinion, what Dad or Mom did, or what the test said you were cut out to be—you'll never be a top accomplisher. You won't be a producer, just a performer. Some day, better now than later, you have to settle on a direction—a cause, a purpose, an anchor, a guiding light. Do it, and it will keep you from wandering a crooked, forever searching path.

When You Have Firm Direction in Your Life . . .

1. Your conflicts lessen and your energy increases. Direction is the best energizer in the world. It's pure magic for motivation, too. As a youth leader I've noticed that once kids have a clear direction and a cause, they'll double their output. My work crews on the job are the same. People who know what they're here for and why, what they want and what they're after, have by far the most energy.

2. You'll have persistence. Staying with it and enduring to the end are essential for any accomplishment in life. It's hard to persist and endure when you don't know what for!

3. You'll save yourself so much time. Once good health is the goal, for example, you don't have to ponder and anguish over menus and exercise opportunities—you know and can get on with it. Firm direction eliminates wavering and wondering.

4. You will beckon and encourage outside help. People are happy to serve and assist those who know what they want and where they're going.

5. You will attract good relationships. Direction radiates stability and we all cling to stable people and places.

6. You'll know when you've reached your goal, so you won't fail to recognize and savor the real accomplishments and rewards in your life.

What about "Charts"?

Once you have your direction—your treasure map—do you post it, file it, or carry it around with you? Where should this vital information be kept—in the head or heart, or on a clipboard in the hand?

The charts that will guide you to your destination in the wide world of doing are your own business, whether they should be big or little, computerized or memorized. I like to write mine down to give them some reality, and I like to share them with others. And as for those goals themselves, try following this simple set of rules when setting them. Your goals should be:

1. Your own—No one else can direct your life or set your goals.
2. Positive, not negative.
3. Ambitious enough to give you a good variety of projects to work on, but not so numerous that you lose focus.
4. Attainable—It's okay to stretch yourself, but your goals must be reachable or you'll lose faith.
5. Exciting!—If what you're about isn't stimulating, alter or change things (yourself, your company, your setting, or your work menu) until it is.
6. Measurable—You need to be able to tell where you are along the way.
7. Tied to a time frame—Establish when you intend to accomplish your goals.

Pick Things That Excite You

At an awards ceremony for a County Home Extension Agents group that I attended, this came across the PA system, word for word:

"And now the next award is for the study of bubble size
in beaten egg whites and its effect on the quality of angel
food cake."

A woman at my table leaned over to another and said sar-
castically, "Lord, is that ever exciting." Personal productivity
really depends on zeroing in on the things that will bring
excitement into *your* life—that's another big rule you have to
follow. If you don't, you're going to spend your time carrying
dead weight around.

The excitement level of things does affect what we produce
on them. When we're excited about someone or something,
we respond with energy and enthusiasm, brain and brawn.
When we're stuck with an unexciting situation (companion
or project), we may stick with it, but we don't do much with
or about it. When you keep things exciting, you keep yourself
highly productive. If you don't like what you're doing, if you
aren't really for the cause or the undertaking, you'll ultimately
only be about 25 percent effective.

When a group of self-made millionaires was analyzed
once to find what they might have in common, it turned out
to be only one thing: They all enjoyed what they did. Their
money basically came from following their hearts. The nice
thing about that is if you follow your heart and make a million bucks, great. If you don't—no problem, you still enjoyed
the journey and that's the reason most of us are out to make a
million in the first place, so we can enjoy ourselves. No one can
decide for you what is exciting; you must decide for yourself.

Personally I couldn't be an accountant in Los Angeles
if you paid me $1,000,000 a year for it and gave me a man-
sion and six months of vacation time. I happen to like out-
door, physical work and could never live in a city. My whole
life, direction, and schedule—from childhood on—has been
attuned to this. But I know friends who wouldn't want their

hands on a hoe handle. It's totally foreign to them; they don't like it, and are uncomfortable with it.

We're all basically the same. If we don't like something, we don't feel productive or happy and so we don't do it. If you hate what you do, but stick to it because you have to (the security, prestige, etc.), you won't ever be a top producer, nor will you reach full potential. If you're simply putting in time, showing up until you can get another position (or waiting for weekends and vacation, relief), this isn't living, and it won't let you produce much either.

If you're in a situation like this, change is an important step to accomplishment. So change the place, the assignment, the activity, the subject, your working partner, or whatever—as long as you're sure it's that thing—that's bogging you down.

If you're not sure whether it's you or the setting, here's a good question to ask yourself: Are there things I will do, night or day, pay or no pay, simply because I like them? Then you do have some productive drive in you! Re-examine your job choices and goals until you find something you can feel that way about.

||||||||||||||||||||||||||||||||||||||||||||||||||||||||||||||||||||||||||||||||||

Notice how we never have trouble getting started
on the things we like to do? Does anyone have
to tell us to start eating a piece of pie, to go
to the beach, to take a luxurious hot bath or
shower? Never! Things we like, we start.

||||||||||||||||||||||||||||||||||||||||||||||||||||||||||||||||||||||||||||||||||

Oddly, many people these days seem to feel it's the company's or boss's responsibility to see to it that they are happy on the job. That's crazy. If you don't enjoy what you do, it's 100 percent your fault—either for staying around, or for not doing something about it and not changing anything. **You** ultimately control your destiny. Maybe not every event that ever happens to you, but at least your attitude and feelings about what you do, where you work, and who you work with.

If you look forward to it, you'll go forward on it—not watching the clock or counting the pay or the credit, but just for the sheer joy of doing.

Focus on Results, Not Efforts

As I was visiting one day with someone who was struggling to "get ahead" in life, she explained her frustrations, especially how discouraged she was about not being able to get around to many of the things she knew needed to be done.

I asked her to make a list of all the things she had to do, and it went like this:

1. Make granddaughter a new dress.
2. Get teeth fixed.
3. Speak at the PTA national conference.
4. Put in the garden.
5. Paint the living room.

6. Tell husband I lost all our vacation money in Las Vegas while at the home show convention!
7. Return waffle iron I borrowed eight years ago (neighbor has forgotten).
8. Go to Seattle to pick up an unfavorite relative.
9. Write that book I've always intended to.

Now the list was logical and intelligent, but just the opposite of how I'd go about it. These are "have to do"-type thoughts and plans, which don't do a thing for motivation. They focus on the work, the effort—the chores instead of the glory. Thinking this way, it's easy to come up with negatives: There really isn't any time to, the machine may not work right, and I don't know what size she is; it'll hurt, I'll feel awful; wonder if they could get someone else, I have nothing to wear; I'll just get it started and a frost will come along and kill everything; I hear paint causes cancer; maybe I should just say I was pickpocketed or leave the country; now that their kids are grown they probably never make waffles; I wonder if I can get sick next week . . . ; I can't spell very well, I'll wait till I get a computer and it will have a spellchecker.

Here's the way I'd rewrite and think of that list:

1. Pick a pattern, choose material for granddaughter's dress. ("Thanks so much for the dress, Grandma, it's so pretty!")
2. Call the dentist for appointment. (Boy, will I look good when he's done, and I'll be able to eat spareribs again.)
3. Select a topic and start researching. Speak to my fellow parents and teachers. ("Tell us more. Hurray, you really helped me!")
4. Buy seed; get ground ready for garden. (Yum, corn on the cob, fresh strawberries, tomatoes, lettuce, watermelons. . . .)

5. Find a paint color that will really set off that room; get a good trim brush. ("That room is such a pleasure to be in now. YOU did it? Yourself?!")

6. Watch for a good mood, figure best time and way to tell husband we're broke. (I can't wait to get that off my chest!)

7. Whip up a batch of my best Belgians and berries and knock on their door and say, "I never like to return a dish empty. . . ." (They'll forgive me anything!)

8. Go to get Aunt Glenda. (Look at the map and figure out an interesting new route to the airport. Get an ice cream on the way. A nice relaxing drive by myself before company gets here!)

9. Get a pad and start jotting down notes for MY book. (The one I've dreamed about. Let's see, I can only spend three weeks in San Francisco signing autographs, one week in France.)

My first reaction to any project is anticipation of the satisfaction and pleasure of the end result. I never think about how much work, money, time, or pain it'll take. I just look at what things will be like when I get done, how good I'll feel, how famous, rich, or loved I'll be. After I relish and bask in that for a while I look at the list again. *Okay, to have a prettier smile and better bite, I'll go see my dentist.*

It's like mothers having babies, pioneers crossing the plains, people entering a marathon, climbing a mountain, cooking, or cleaning—if you look at it too long or dwell on the immediate inconvenience, pain, or risk, you'll never get started. Or, once you do start, you'll be timidly and reluctantly committed. How many pioneers would have left the comfort of their homes if they'd dwelt on the fact that they were going to freeze, sweat, starve, suffer, and maybe lose some members of their party on the way? They focused and decided on having their own land, the fruits of that land, and freedom.

This is a secret that most highly productive people use. They don't get lost in the paperwork and footwork, the details of getting there, but plan and prepare for the cause, the result, the REWARD.

High Producers Don't Ignore the Rules!

Oh boy, now come the sticky fingers on the steering wheel of direction: Even direction is regulated by rules. There have to be rules for the road, boundary lines, start and stop signals, dos and don'ts, times and seasons. Society, like nature, has to follow laws or it won't function. Selling rules to anyone can be a long, tough process. One of the first things babies and children learn in life is how to operate by the rules. As people grow older they often feel they have exemptions and can become disillusioned with rules. We've all wanted to skip or ignore rules that interfere with our path or method, intentions or schedule.

Someone once said, "Obedience is the first law of heaven." I say, **"Following the rules, not making your own, is the first law of successful direction."** Consider the carefully constructed Constitution of our country, health and safety rules, the rules of sound financing, and the rules of the road, for instance. Rules exist to enable things to work smoothly, to protect and enhance us, and to help us attain our goals and follow our direction. If you doubt that, you only have to stand back and observe that the most calm and efficient people, the high producers, are those who follow the rules, and those who make their own rules are the strugglers and stress-sufferers.

Sure, you have the freedom to obey or follow the rules or not, but you don't have freedom from the consequences. And those consequences can foul up a life as well as a project or agenda. Remember, too, that you can follow the rules and still have your own values, set your own style and timetable, and pick your own places and companions.

Do Your OWN Planning and Preparation

In life, we all do a lot of jumping out into space and into places and situations we've never been before. If I ever had the nerve to jump out of an airplane at 5,000 feet, I'd want to pack my own parachute because I know how much the outcome depends on how, when, and if that chute works on the way down. The only way to have any control and confidence is to be as well prepared as possible for what's coming. And no one knows the preparations needed as well as you do. You know how much you're likely to eat, drink, sleep, and sweat, how much you can lift and tolerate, how well you can see and hear, what your allergies are, what you can't do without, who you want to travel with.

Don't let *them* (committees, the folks, bosses, statistics, spouses) decide for you and don't let just anyone pack your chute. You don't know if it would be a Monday morning or Friday afternoon chute—if they did it when they were fresh and sharp and alert, or worn down, tired, and distracted. Do your own planning; don't depend on *them* to do it for you. Committees are poor planners—they're fine for reviewing and readjusting, but a bad source of original planning and preparation.

You need to do it yourself. Tailor the trip to fit your talents, temperament, energy, and level of commitment. When someone else packs your lunch, suitcase, briefcase, or diaper bag, you just have to get by with what's been given to you when it's time to eat, dress, or address the project. Whether it's what you needed or wanted or not, whether it works or not—that's all you've **got!**

I see thousands of high school students asking others, "What do you think I should do for a living? Where should I work? What should I study?" Getting input and advice is good, but letting people actually organize, plan and prepare for you, and choose your direction for you, can be as crippling as letting someone else buy your shoes.

Do your own planning. Use others' ideas and checklists if they help, but make your own adaptations of them. Scan your own brain and then pack your own bag. That's one big secret of being highly productive.

Lists

I have lists, I use lists, I love lists—but lists don't make you do anything. Lists don't change anything; they don't inspire; they don't necessarily organize you much either. They're just a record so you won't forget what you have to do. Take a grocery list, for example. Your memory is taxed less, and you have less chance of forgetting something, if you have everything you need written down there, so you can see it and check things off as you get them. If you start expecting a list to save or discipline you, to prioritize your life and assignments, to make you reach goals simply because you've listed them—forget it. It'll be your downfall.

Likewise, don't take the order on lists too seriously. The president of a big *Fortune* 500 company said he had the answer for accomplishment: "Just make a list. Put the most important things on the top and don't go on to number two until number one is done." This is one of the most counterproductive approaches I've ever heard of.

What if something needed to accomplish number four on the list was missing, so you got hung up for a couple of days? What about new, more pressing things that crop up an hour after you've made the list? You prioritize to the situation, not to the list.

Let's look at an example of this. You have two seemingly similar project managers. They have the same general abilities and education; however, one is efficient and performs her job adequately, while the other is highly efficient and does phenomenally. Why? Both have lists and both have schedules and duties for the day—then (as it always will) some surprise thing comes up, something unimportant. The efficient project manager adds it neatly and logically to her list of things to do, after the last thing she listed this morning. The effective manager looks at the new chore, scans her list, and places it wherever it will get done the fastest and the best. She ignores order and protocol, the clock, and previously established priorities, because maybe taking care of the new task right then will only take five minutes and if she waits until later, until its logical place on the list, it will take two hours.

No great accomplisher or producer ever operates with a rigid list—it will throttle freedom and flexibility.

Who's Afraid of the Big Bad List?

As for the size of your list of "to-dos," the bigger, the better! Don't hesitate to put it all down, even the impossible dreams and the know-I-can't-get-to-it-yet items.

At one time I had over 6,000 to-dos on my list, and several thousand of them are done now, too. It's heartening to believe and know that a man or woman is capable of doing not merely 6,000 things, but an unlimited number. The more the merrier, and the more items on your to-do list (as long as they are things you really want or need to do), the better position you'll be in to change tasks to fit your mood and momentum.

If you eliminate things from your list simply because the list seems to be getting long, both you and they lose a chance at the time slot that will always pop up in a down time, or the spaces that come along every day when we least expect them. Just quit trying to assign a time to every to-do item; instead, let them slide into the time in your life when they happen to fit.

Try distributing your lists to your family or hanging them up for others to see. **One of the best ways to get things done is to make your path public,** because then others will jump in and help you, and you can help others.

The best list wisdom is to carry your list with you at all times. Keep it in plain sight or accessible, and look at it often!

Which Priority Takes Precedence?

How can one master the art of juggling priorities? How do you figure out which "need to do this NOW" is number one on your list when you're being pulled and pressed in all directions? This has nothing to do with ability, I assure you—you already have the ability. The real battle here is about values. If you have clear direction in what you're doing, priorities are a mere matter of selecting and organizing your activities for the day. If you're having problems with priorities, you'd better examine (or re-examine and reaffirm) where you are going and why. Once that's figured out, your priorities will be, too.

Make Sure It's Worth the Time

For many years my company has contracted the cleaning and maintenance of public phone booths. Simple as these units are, there are several levels of service you can give them. The first is what we might call the "lick-and-promise" level, and it would only take about five minutes and cost $5.00 per booth, but the level of cleanliness would be unsatisfactory. The other extreme of maintenance, the "gold-plate" level, would take at least an hour and cost $20 or $25 a booth. Even if it is affordable, the gold plate going-over wouldn't make sense because of the rapid deterioration of the phone booth from weather and usage. A middle-level job, a good commercial cleaning, would take about fifteen or twenty minutes. It would keep the booths clean, fresh, and pleasant to use, and only cost about $10 to $15 a booth. Going further than that and polishing all the outside metal, plastic, and glass to diamond brilliance would be a waste of time, because within hours the finish would oxidize, waterstain, and be handprinted all over and look no better than the less expensive commercial job that serves the purpose. Gold-plating would take four times as long and cost four or five times as much and really benefit no one.

The same is true of sweeping a floor. One minute after the job is finished, dust, dirt, and crumbs begin to build up again. It would be pretty silly to start over to resweep the floor the minute you finish, because a reasonable level of cleanliness will do, and that is what you're really after.

In all of your projects, think this through and allocate your time according to the value of the undertaking. Standards are a pivotal part of any project, and you have to pick yours if you are going to be a producer.

Reverse Those Big and Little Projects

We seldom have anything "medium" to do. Once we've settled on a direction, our projects, chores, and goals seem to be either big ones or little ones and we shape and engrave them in our minds as such. Then, 99 percent of us have the impulse to attack, work on, and finish at least forty-four little projects before getting at the big one. It's a kind of avoidance ailment. Even if the big one is far more important (which it usually is), we warm up to, prepare ourselves for, and stay immersed in the little ones, and as we do that the big one looms over us ever more menacingly.

Why do we do this? "Big" usually does mean more work and commitment and a loss of some flexibility to leave work early. But the real reasons run deeper. Big projects usually involve some big-picture thinking (which means *real* thinking, which we tend to avoid). They often involve some change as well, so we want to put them off as long as possible. And the risks are bigger with big projects; we aren't so sure that we'll succeed with them.

Maybe it seems easier to you to love the little things and avoid the big ones. The opposite is actually true. **Doing the big project first is generally not just faster, but easier on us mentally and physically.** The price—in time, money, guilt, worry, trouble, and delayed progress—of even one undone big project weighs us down every day of our lives, through every one of those little projects we keep doing to avoid the big one.

Big doesn't always mean long, either. One of the greatest mistakes we all make in production is in putting off those one-day (or one-hour) jobs or projects that will bless and affect our whole lives from that moment forward. We dodge them and keep transferring them from list to list, even for five or ten years or even longer.

Just for fun, do a reverse. For a month, forget the little projects (keep them on a list somewhere, but don't do any of them or even think about them). Instead, tackle a couple of the major projects that you've pushed aside for a while now. You'll have the immediate satisfaction of dealing with some

important overdue issues. And by the time you finish those big projects you'll notice that many of the little ones on your list will be gone, automatically sandwiched in with or solved by the big one.

With a bit of practice you can always take advantage of the fact that most big projects have pockets of time in which you can do little projects at the same time. Being involved in one thing doesn't mean we have to forgo doing other things. Direction can have a thousand paths to its destination.

Don't Let Schedules Be Shackles

The word "scheduling" has a fascination for the time-management-minded, but you really don't have to know much about scheduling to get a lot done. Schedules will bind and stiffen you if you follow them too closely. People who have become such expert schedulers that they run around with a planner in their hand at all times lose creativity and flexibility—the schedule becomes their master. So much time is wasted, for example, when something that's been scheduled is canceled because of rain, illness, or whatever. Everyone loses at least half a day spinning their wheels and mentally retooling. Scheduling also has a way of inhibiting ambition and action—it shifts our brain out of "what if" gear.

Scheduling is necessary for harmony and compatibility in public matters or group efforts, and a must for teamwork, classes, appointments, and the like. But in my own undertakings, I prefer as much as possible to be able to respond and react to options. Rigid schedules take the fun out of life and leave no room for adventure. Whenever I can, I work to a *standard*, not a schedule. A schedule might tell us to clean all the corners once a week, on every Tuesday. A standard tells us to keep the corners clean, and that means clean them when they need cleaning, which might be next week or next month. A schedule runs your clock and calendar, while a standard leaves room for flow and mood and opportunity. Good scheduling for me is having a big frontlog (see page 92) and then going with the flow, not being controlled by the clock or the calendar.

My wife and I, for example, purchased some property on Kauai (the garden isle of Hawaii) and started a long-term project of designing and building a maintenance-free house. One winter, we squared away our personal and business affairs and left for Hawaii for a while. I took some manuscripts and new book ideas and a list of forty other things to do in the two months we planned on staying—gardening and landscaping work, visiting with friends there, and building the house were our main objectives. There was no predetermined order or attempt to put things into time slots on the list; it was simply a list of objectives.

The first morning was sunny. My wife and I went out, unscheduled, into the yard and had a ball whaling away at weeds all day. We didn't stop to eat at regular times, just worked on the task to our hearts' content. We did the same the next day, started feeling "in shape," and decided that this might be a good plan for the next five days. **We didn't schedule it but we did prepare for it.**

Then the rains came—rain like you've never seen. Our house is six miles from Mt. Wiaialiai, the wettest spot on earth (more than 400 inches of rain a year). For three days, we had nonstop rain—all day and night. I selected (totally unscheduled) one of the book topics, the one that fit my mood, and in four days drafted a book. About that time I received a call from a national TV network producer who offered me a slot as a regular guest, and wanted some help with segment ideas. I took two or three days and wrote up the scripts (again, totally unscheduled). I even traveled to New York for a couple of days. Two more phone calls diverted me to other important activities and I rolled them right into my week and went on. All of this was fun, fast, and exciting. If I'd been following a "schedule," I would only have accomplished about half of what I did, and I'd have been constantly caught up in the confusion of rescheduling. Rigid scheduling is usually unproductive.

Be Careful with "Budgeting" Time

As for setting aside or budgeting a day or a block of time for a certain project—top producers don't do it that way.

If you say, "I'm going to use next weekend to clean out the garage," and you block or schedule or set aside that time for it, you'll stretch the task out and use up that much time whether you actually need it or not. You can choose to spend two whole days on this or more realistically and efficiently half a day, depending on how much of a project you want to make out of it.

Often, too, jobs we dread or that aren't quite our cup of tea become magnified in our minds, so we overestimate how much time will be required for them. There was a giant pile of press clippings, for example, in a corner of the office for the longest time because everyone shuddered at the thought of how long it would take to sort and file them all. When someone finally faced up to it, three years' worth of accumulation and dread (which we imagined would easily take three days) was disposed of in three hours. If that someone had blocked out three days to do the job, it probably would've taken that long.

You may run into the opposite problem with your pre-selected block of time—it turns out to be too small for the project slotted there, so you end up deep in guilt, with a chain reaction of block reshuffling, reassignment, and apologies.

Designating days or certain stretches of time for jobs is a limiting approach and a confession of not being able to control more than one thing at a time.

The fun in life is in beating the clock, not letting the clock regulate you and your projects. Do all you can, as fast as you can—and don't get too hung up on the WHEN.

"Should I Do It in Order?" Not Always!

One of the biggest struggles people have with direction is that they think it might reduce their freedom, thwart creativity, and dampen thrills, and that it offers no flexibility, etc. Not so! Direction is only a committed choice, a goal, a chosen route or course—not a straitjacket. If, on the way someone burns your bridges, you hit a storm, or you run out of steam, you have 110 options to go under, over, around, or through to reach your goal. The only important part is to keep holding course to the lighthouse you are heading for. Direction isn't a total allegiance to any order; it's not a stern, unyielding system. Direction may need to be an undeviating course, but it isn't a straight, rigid line.

Just watch super-producers work. You don't have to start with number one and then go to number two, or work from top to bottom or from front to back. When they film movies and commercials they seldom do it in order. They may shoot the end first, the middle last, and the first part in the middle! You'd think it would be confusing, but I've experienced it and it actually goes twice as fast because they are concentrating on efficiency. **There are no hard and fast rules for an efficient order of completing things.** Order is often how something best organizes itself, not how we organize it.

That's why high producers don't like to have too many people involved in their activities, because they can't always chart the exact number of people they'll need, or plot the exact sequence or order of things. If the mood hits them, they get in a rhythm or on a roll; they may shoot off in what seems like an entirely different direction but in fact they're holding course with their overall directional setting all the time. They'll jump around on projects or change something right in the middle of the most important part. And they often establish order during, not before!

Course Correction

One of my baseball teammates was pitching his best game ever. He'd held the other team to a standstill and was cruising through the last inning. With a runner on first, he began his wind-up but knocked his hat down over his eyes, instantly eliminating his view of the entire field—including the batter he was throwing to. As you may know, once a pitcher has started to throw to a batter, he can't stop the motion. If he does, it is a "balk," and the runner can advance a base. The balking rule came immediately to my friend's mind and so he didn't stop his motions but proceeded to throw the ball blindly (but softly) in the direction of the batter. The batter, of course, slugged the life out of the ball, and the runner, instead of getting one base, got around to home and they won the game.

In "made an error" situations like this we usually have more time to think things through than this pitcher did. Even so, because we are already in motion we often let a simple need for course correction become a crash.

It is a hard thing to do, to stop and adjust things and take a loss of time or progress in the process. But course correction, when it's called for, is the wisest of all courses for even the fastest mover. It may feel like backtracking but it isn't; it's just getting back on track, and it saves a lot of time in the long run.

The Fuller Brush plant has a reputation for making magnificent, high-quality brushes. When I visited, I saw a whole trashcan full of beautiful wood handles. I lifted out some of those fine polished handles on their way to being made into sawdust and could barely find a blemish on them. The workers there said that it was hard at first to dispose of something, or completely redo it, because of one little flaw or weakness. But at the end of the line where other parts and the reputation of 10,000 other brushes had to depend on the strength and quality of the one, it made sense.

Maybe you've had this experience. You're putting in a big beam, even riveting one into a building, and you pause for a moment to check your progress and notice that the beam is a little crooked. You don't want to stop, pull it out, and redo your work, but if you don't, you'll be building on a crooked base, so realignment only makes sense.

This is the toughest discipline of all for many people, stopping the momentum of a great work to correct a tiny error. Good producers do it.

"You Can't Serve Two Masters"—Can You?

That old saying about serving two masters is true, but it's talking about allegiance and direction, not duties. **When it comes to simply tasks, you can do two or ten or a hundred at the same time.** One person can have twenty-two tops going at once, another can keep fifteen kites flying. Some people play five instruments at the same time, and innovative fishermen can tend to thirteen rods. And thousands and thousands of farmers grow half a dozen different crops at the same time.

If you make an activity your master, you can only serve one at a time. If you stay the master, you can multiply at will. We all play multiple roles simultaneously—aunt, sister, husband, brother-in-law, cousin, grandparent, lawyer, fisherman, lover, painter, etc. Just because one thing is going on doesn't mean that everything else has to stop. You don't watch a tree grow after you've planted it; that's unproductive. If you plant hundreds of things, with some nurturing they will grow and you can be doing other things at the same time.

I started a cleaning museum about ten years ago, and have a pretty nice collection now although I haven't spent much time "collecting." While doing other things—speaking, traveling, calling, writing, visiting—I'd mention it to people and tell them what I was looking for and how enthused I was about the project, asking them to spread the word, too. In time things started to come in, and they've kept on coming!

Top Time Thieves

You want to do more and do better, and you want more time. The gang of time thieves you have to contend with includes overdoing, overdebating, and failing to go all the way and commit yourself. All of the following thrive in an atmosphere of little or no direction.

Overkill

Over- anything generally undoes the objective—overeating, overheating, overloading, overpacking, overcleaning, overstaying.

A husband and wife in my community, for example, were each assigned a ten-minute talk for a church meeting. The moment they accepted, everything else in life went on hold for the next two weeks. They spent hours and hours studying and preparing—all for a simple ten-minute talk. An informal presentation isn't worth two weeks of work; there isn't a balance there. That much preparation wasn't necessary, even if they had the time to spare for it. And unfortunately, all of this effort kept them from accepting again, so they never had a chance to learn to do it faster and better.

Interpersonal relationships are important to us all, but even social niceties can be overdone. My company, Varsity Contractors, is pretty big now, and across my desk come cards for birthdays, weddings, and such. I sign the cards and route them on down the line. A while ago a thank-you card thanking us for sending a card arrived on my desk. Can you believe it—a thank-you note for a thank-you note we had sent, and it had been through ten departments already! If I hadn't stopped it, there would have been fifty departments thanking them for thanking us for thanking them.

Likewise, I did a good deed for a woman while on a road trip once. It cost me nothing and helped her a lot and I felt good about it. A week later came an elaborate thank-you note and some goodies, so of course I wrote back a thank-you note for her goodies. Now she sent me some pictures of her family and asked, would I please send them back after I had a chance to look them over, and I did. Then she sent me another thank-you note for sending them back, and at least one more round followed. The correspondence had to end—I have tons of mail to answer every week!

A well-directed person can do half a dozen projects while his or her counterpart overkills one. Things worth doing aren't *always* worth doing well; sometimes just getting the job done is enough! Going on and on in an activity can cause the result to slip over from a positive to a negative. Even useful, productive things became unproductive when they're overdone.

Overkill can be cured simply and easily by always knowing where and what the finish line is, and by having clear direction before you start. Learn to cut off activities when your inner instinct tells you they're finished. **"Stop" and "done" are easy to see if you look before you leap into an activity.** Decide what the finish point is, and no matter how things are going when you get there, stop. Overkill is a waste of time and money and usually a pain to the recipient, too—the one whom we intended to please with all that extra effort.

Overanalyzing

In sports and political arenas, people spend hours and months of their time on polls and predictions that don't change anything or mean a thing until the game is played or vote is held. Rehashing past events will never change the outcome of games or political gains, either. It's pretty dumb unless you're an analyst who is getting paid to make predictions, or unless you have some real use for these speculations.

On a business trip, I was flipping the dial on the hotel TV and observed a total of twenty-two channels—seventeen of them presenting various people hard at work analyzing, projecting, hashing, and rehashing. What could happen?

And what if it did—then what would happen? What might happen if the present trend continued? What could have happened instead of what did happen? Not one solid bit of actual reality.

Nonproducers are always reporting, analyzing, evaluating, or discussing what has happened or might happen instead of making things happen. They're always kicking through the ruins of the fire speculating, instead of cleaning it up and starting a new building. Second-guessing like this has no value and can change nothing. Meddling, opinionating, and deciding for other people will only cut into your own fun time and progress. Getting into the affairs of others will only keep you from go-getting.

Don't sit around waiting for someone else to tell you how things are, have been, and will be. Few real producers get too hung up on statistics. That just corrals your creativity and lines you up instead of letting you set your own lines. Your goal is to make your own statistics!

Delayed Decision-Making

Indecisive people are never high producers. Learn to make decisions not with "maybe" or "I'll see," but a resounding one-time "I will!" More and more of us are having our direction set and our decisions made for us by the company, the government, the county, the city, the counselor. Even well-qualified and educated people just coast along; it's easier, safer, and handier to let someone else decide and then go along with it. There's lots of name and job protection in letting others do the deciding.

You can't just educate yourself into high production; the moment of decision to put the principles into action, instead of just learning more about them, has to come. Some training and even inspiration is often necessary before making the decision, but this isn't time wasted. But the decision is where the ball game really starts—all the rest is practice.

So make that decision, and mean it:

- I'm never going to break training.
- I will be on time.
- I will work nine hours a day for the next year.

The biggest battle of go-getting ends the minute you decide to stop brooding, stalling, and analyzing, and just DO the job at hand. Trying it out, thinking about it, or considering it won't accomplish anything except confusion and discouragement. Doers decide and *do*. The average person can't even decide to decide, and so average people remain average. Most of us have the equipment and power to travel well in life. Few of us do, however, because we won't commit to a direction and get started on it. It's like an automobile—if you leave it in neutral, you can rev the motor full-blast, burn a lot of gas, make a lot of noise, and eventually wear the motor out, but you'll never move. And when you don't move, people will:

- Run over you
- Push you
- Pull you

. . . where they want to go, not where you intended or wanted to go!

Decision does put you at risk to some degree, but have you noticed all the high producers and go-getters are willing to take risks?

> *"How did you get so successful?"*
> "Good judgment."
> *"How did you get good judgment?"*
> "Experience."
> *"How did you get experience?"*
> "Bad judgment."

Confidence comes from conquering. How do you get lots done? You decide, and then handle the problem or the demand. Even if you foul it up a few times before you get it right, you are producing or on the road to production—something that can't be done just on the planning board or in a dream.

For the next week or so, watch the go-getters when a situation arises. They will react to it, stew, storm, or smile about it, hesitate for a moment or maybe a few minutes, and then make a decision. They don't expect perfection or guarantee instant success; they just say, "This is what I will do," and amazing things happen. Even if the decision was dead wrong, somehow the go-getters surge ahead, adapt to and fix the situation, and end up with a good score.

Notice, too, how no one gives much help to an indecisive person. How can you help an indecisive person, if you don't know what he or she is about? Once a decision is made everyone jumps in and helps. Some may criticize and fight the decision, but all in all there is action and progress, and something productive is in the making!

A farmer I know said, "When you get started, you're half done." That old fellow had it figured out. Think about your own life: How many times have you dreaded doing something—put it off, avoided it, sidestepped it thirty times, burned up acres of energy worrying about it, analyzed it for hours on end? Then, once you decided and jumped in, the task took only hours to complete. First you were flooded with relief, then the second wave came: "Gadfrey, I could have done this four years ago and saved weeks of my life."

Think of all the people you know, and the differences between those who've never done anything wrong because they never took a chance or risk nor tried anything, and those who step out ahead of everyone else. When horses all run together in a big dust cloud it doesn't rattle anyone's emotions. People cheer when one of those horses breaks out of the pack and surges ahead. People who venture forth and expand their lives are more loved and interesting than those who just stay holed up. Lengthen your stride, magnify your calling, and accomplish a lot, and you'll end up blessing other lives along with your own.

Doers Don't Try, They Do

> We have a poster here in our office that says:
> *If you ever use the word "try" around here . . .*
> *you are automatically fired!*

Listen to top producers—you'll seldom or never hear the word "try." How would you react to a pilot who told you he was going to "try" to fly the plane you were on? Or a surgeon who, just before operating on you, said, "Well, I'll **try**." Or a boss who promised to "try" to pay you for your work?

When someone says, "I'll try to get this done for you," what does that tell you? Nothing! Even saying "I tried my very best" means little when it comes to production. Doers don't try, they do or they don't do. "Try" and "decide" can't be used in the same sentence!

The Right Roads Are Right in Front of Us

Wandering scholars of the past collected answers to "the secret meaning of life." In today's overextended society, we wander in a rather desperate search for the secrets to getting more done.

Over the years, I've compiled my own little list of secrets, picked up along the way from experience, and from talking to the mountain-movers of today and watching them operate. These ideas aren't new; in fact, they are so available, common, and free that we often overlook them in grasping for something novel or profound.

1. Obey Your Own Experience and Instinct!

Follow your first impulse. Without any conscious effort, we can all come up with a sound, efficient course of action for ourselves. We are born with this "automatic transmission" of the mind. Learning to follow these feelings requires some experience, some humility, and some discipline, but it's a wonderful way to set your compass. So listen to the inner ticking that talks to you. The wisdom and promptings of the spirit inside us are a gift we all have that we don't use enough.

2. Believe History

Too often our main interest in history has been to get a grade from it or be entertained by it. Yet nothing is plainer and more accurate than a simple look at the record to see how millions of others made out with their directions. Wouldn't we be dumb to repeat the actions of those who ran off the road? As individuals, we can get pure, truthful intelligence from history. And we can pick the prime movers of the past to pattern our own lives after. But few do it.

3. Wise People

Not smart, but wise people. Those who lived and produced wonderment during "their time," for example, knew a lot about time. What they did and how and why they did it is worth copying. Don't parrot a personality—just pattern a procedure, maybe readjust your route to match one they used to do something faster and better. This is kind of like following "individual history."

Time to Take a Break

Now for a refresher on why we want to do more. Sure, it's fun, rewarding, and profitable, but there are a couple of other very good reasons to do it. . . .

- It's great PR. Selling yourself and your causes, purposes, wants, and needs to others is key to keeping all of your goals and projects headed toward accomplishment. Doing a lot does a lot of broadcasting of its own.
- Doing more is good communication! Being in touch with others adds a lot to our lives, and doing does this automatically for you.
- Doing gives you social security. Not a reserve of cash to be disbursed later, but a reserve, a stockpile, of ever more interesting and worthwhile things to do.

Chapter 5
The Magic of Early

In reviewing all of my notes and research for this book and trying to figure out the bottom line, the near-perfect solution to doing more, nothing profound popped up besides the usual "hard work, persistence, follow-up"—all those familiar success keys that we change the names of every year or so. I didn't find the secret to my own success until I was sitting in an executive committee meeting of my cleaning company one day. I was listening to the bosses report on recently developed problems throughout the many states we operate in. As I listened, I began to jot a one-word reason or summary beside each. I found myself writing late, late, behind, late, forgot, late.

Later that evening, I was visiting at a friend's house when a panicked phone call came in regarding a school assignment. **The reason for the hustle and hurry? Again, lateness.**

In the headquarters of a mail-order company the next morning, I eavesdropped on ten incoming calls and the scrambling around and apologizing that followed—five of the ten calls were the result of lateness.

Before observing these situations, lateness really hadn't occurred to me as the villain of the day. So to double-check I ran over to my corporate office and asked eleven executives—CPAs, safety officers, managers, etc.—what percentage of their calls and correspondence that day had to do with problems. "Sixty-five percent," was the answer. What was their one-word summary of the cause for most of those problems? You guessed it: people being *late*.

I had it! The most important principle for getting more done, the "solve most" word in the vocabulary of accomplishment:

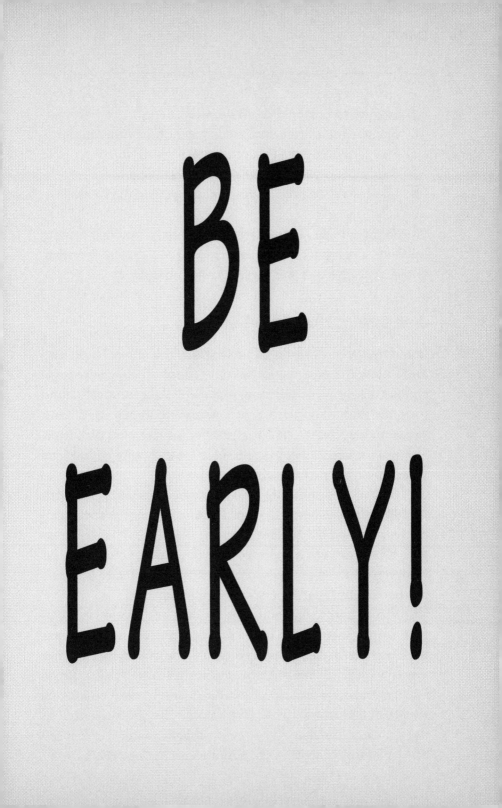

The early bird got much, much more than the worm.

1. She got the first choice of morsels.
2. She got the admiration and respect of the other birds.
3. She got good press and publicity.
4. She got "no sweat" comfort and relaxation.
5. She got the rest of the day to do anything she wanted.

While all the late birds hunted, dug, scratched, fought, lined up, negotiated, made excuses, prayed, hoped, crowded, and shoved, the early bird was getting more done!

Just Look at What Early Eliminates

If you follow just one bit of advice from this entire book, read and follow the next few pages. The simple, inexpensive principle of being early will single-handedly, automatically (and for no cost and little effort) prevent about 80 percent of your "time management," personal, and organizational problems. Doing more early will also increase your quality of life by a wonderfully predictable amount.

By being early in life, you carry a competency flag with you. The flag waves to all of the world a message that you can be depended upon. Lateness, on the other hand, is like dragging a ball and chain, announcing to all that you are always bringing up the rear and cannot totally be trusted to be there, no matter how good a person you may be.

Victor Borge, the famous comedian and world-class pianist, summed it up one night during a performance. He was well into his routine when a woman came in late, fighting her way through the rows to her seat near the front. Borge stopped playing and the woman proceeded to trample over people, rustling and disturbing her way to her seat. Borge apologized to the audience (much to the woman's chagrin, as all eyes focused on her ill-timed arrival), "Excuse me, excuse me, excuse me."

After she sat down, he walked over near to where she was now sitting and said, "Where are you from, ma'am?"

"Fifty-Seventh Street," she replied.

"Well, lady, I'm from Denmark and I was here on time."

People are much more irritated by late than we ever know; it can dampen everything from promotions and raises to sexual desire. Late people crowd us physically and mentally. We all hate the fact that their lateness undoes our schedule and disrupts our day. Showing up late for work or sending something in late, no matter how well it's finally done, still means a mark against you.

When to Prepare? Early!

There's no such thing as too far ahead. I have speeches, appointments, and projects scheduled for 2006 through 2008, and although this is only 2005, as soon as the times and the topics are set, I start preparing for those presentations and projects, collecting notes and ideas. I do it over the course of the year. It takes almost zero time, and I end up with a choice speech or whatever with little time or cost in it. If I waited until the night or even the week before, then I'd have to spend hours hunting, making calls, and sitting down and studying. When you spread your preparation out over time, the work almost does itself!

It's easy to start incorporating early preparation. Next time you have a trip coming up, don't pack the night before. Set your bag or suitcase out and drop things in it over the course of the week before your trip. That way, you'll never be in a last-minute rush, and you'll seldom forget anything. And you won't be up at midnight picking out clothes and ideas the night before the trip.

My dad ran a ranch four times bigger than any of the neighbors' without any hired help. Now I realize why he was so good at it. We never went to bed one night without knowing exactly what we were going to be doing the next day. The tools for tomorrow were always lined up and laid out. Our equipment and machinery was ready six months before our neighbors,' who waited to inspect their equipment until the very week they needed it. Needed parts took weeks to arrive and in the meantime the neighbors lost sleep, crops, and schedules. My family had plenty of lead time, so if we came upon a problem we were able to handle it easily.

Being ready in advance is fun and comforting. As a boy, one of my jobs was feeding the cattle. It took fifteen minutes to muscle the bales up to the mangers, and only about three minutes to feed. I dreaded rounding up the bales, especially when

I was in a rush. So right after the evening feeding, I'd round up the bales for the morning and place them right near the mangers. This way, if it was cold or windy, or if I was running late or had a ball game, I could get feeding done in three minutes instead of eighteen. It always feels good to work in advance, to have something done ahead, to be ready, just in case.

Work Ahead, Not Behind

Observe high producers, and you'll notice the word "later" seldom issues from their lips. Sure, we do always have to "squeeze something into the schedule," and even the best producer has moments of weakness, of not feeling quite up to doing something right now. Anything slated "to do later," however, is at great risk of ending up on one of those "unresolved" piles that so many of us have in our lives. We've stacked this stuff in line to get to, but haven't gotten to it yet. It's kind of like putting things in a little fix-it or do-it hospital and then not attending to them. They just fill up all the beds in our brain and have to be fed and looked after to keep them alive. And they seldom heal themselves.

Most "later" things end up taking more energy, aggravation, and worry than just doing them right away ever would. When a neglected fifteen-minute job goes stale it suddenly becomes a two-hour nightmare accompanied by unnecessary emotional wear and tear.

Consider the building inspector who told the owners of a building to get the roof repaired. They had an estimate done and it came to $5,000. They didn't want to spend that much right then, so they waited two years. By then the water had ruined the walls, floors, doors, and the support beams. The fixing cost two years later was $50,000! The owners first saw the leak when it was $15 to fix . . . and waited.

Make working ahead and early your style; convert all those "later's" to "now's" and you'll be ten times as efficient.

Being in front of and ahead of things is much more inspiring than always being behind, digging your way out. There is a whole different feeling to being the aggressor, looking ahead and doing ahead, rather than forever fighting and patching up problems that should have been handled a long time ago.

The time to get things done is when they can be done most quickly, cheaply, and enjoyably. That is almost always *early*.

|||||||||||||||||||||||||||||||||||||||||||||||||||||||||||||||||||||||||||||||||||||||||||||

Toss "later" out of your vocabulary right along
with the word "try." Along with "later" we have
to carry the vague burden of "when." Even
"See you later" has a built-in "When?"

|||||||||||||||||||||||||||||||||||||||||||||||||||||||||||||||||||||||||||||||||||||||||||||

Keep a Frontlog, Not a Backlog

Ninety percent of people keep and use backlogs—lists of work to do or things that should be done once they're caught up on the daily list of things to do.

High producers don't have backlogs. When you work from behind you never really catch up. Producers maintain a "frontlog," a list of things to do ahead. When you're always working ahead of yourself, pushing things ahead of you rather than pulling them behind you, you have twice the control.

Just how do you assemble a frontlog? I can use some buzzwords and tell you to be proactive instead of reactive, or ask you to be active rather than passive, but often telling people to "be" this or that can be futile. Out of all the "be's" preached and commanded and suggested, however, there is one truly easy and self-rewarding behavior. It is the indisputable Number One in learning to get more done, as well as the exact way to create a frontlog. What is this biggest "be" in the books of accomplishment? **BE EARLY**, of course!

Type up your frontlog and carry it with you always. Then make little swipes and snips at it as you can, as the mood strikes and opportunities small, medium, and large appear. If you keep consistently chipping away at it like this, gradually the original projects will be done and disappear, and fresh new to-do "twigs and branches" will appear on your log.

Remember, productive people always have a bigger list of things to do, not a smaller one, as life goes on—that's what makes doing more worth the effort.

What Time of Day Is Best for Doing?

There is only one right answer to this question: early. For me, the morning hours will always out-produce the evening hours three to one. I do all my finely tuned mental stuff (such as writing) in the wee morning hours. When my brain dies, I make calls and run errands, write letters, etc. When body and brain both die, I hit (in the early evening) the physical stuff and work with a pitchfork or shovel. Then I use the "overtime" (late) hours in the day to lay things out for the morning, so that I can hit the road running, not getting myself together to get started.

Another reason early is often the best time to do the most ambitious things is that by the time we get through all of the chores and duties of the day, we're usually too out of time and energy to tackle any of the big stuff, the main or real agenda. **When to get the most done, however, is a strictly personal decision.** Regulate this yourself; don't let me or anyone else (other than possibly your boss!) dictate the time of day in which you do most of your accomplishing.

We might all use the same clock, but there are no rules as to which part of it we choose to use the hardest—it could be the left or right side or the bottom or somewhere in the middle. Do keep other people's clocks in mind, though. Otherwise your project may come screeching to a halt because you need a part, supply, or consultation with someone who sticks to the old 9 to 5!

We're all different, so find a fit (your fit—not that of any author or consultant) and follow it.

Early Eliminates Deadline Stress

"Early" has the power to eliminate another ugly time-stealer from your life: deadlines. The word "deadline" is seldom used by a super-producer.

People who only work to deadlines are survivors, not doers. Deadlines can serve as a crutch for the weak-willed and unmotivated. If you're working for the deadline, and not the completion of the project or task, you lose the joy in accomplishment. People who are all hung up on deadlines will ruin your nerves and work less efficiently than anyone around. Deadline people are the ones who invented and need overnight delivery. Deadline people have a habit of starting a day late instead of a day early and this cuts them out of any new or priority things that might come up by way of opportunity.

A deadline becomes your stalker the minute you set it. The name alone—"dead-line"—ought to tell you something. If you are early (no extra cost; no strain; no explanations) you don't have to worry about deadlines.

Waiting—Give It a Shot of Early

The average American spends more than five years of his or her life waiting.

If you sometimes wonder why you can't seem to get much done, add up your time waiting not just in traffic but to: eat, pay, check in, check out, go to the bathroom, get the mail, catch a cab, be admitted, get what you ordered, be seen at your appointment with the doctor/lawyer, etc. Just about any attempt to do anything seems to get us caught up in some waiting time. So:

1. Avoid waiting whenever you can, by going early or at off times or not going at all. And, whenever possible, avoid people who keep you waiting every time.

2. Prepare so that you can use waiting time productively. Carry some work (that you've prepared earlier) with you all the time. (See page 128.) If you enjoy your work as you should, this is like carrying a tennis racket or your knitting around.

Fixing—Do It Early

None of us is exempt from the need to fix things, but we do have a choice of when to fix them. I came to this realization the hard way. One of the rear tires on my seminar van was getting

bald. It almost cried out, "Change me! Change me!" as it went around—but I didn't fix it. I was holding out, hoping to get just "one more trip" out of it. On the way to Los Angeles, deep in the heart of the Nevada desert, the tire blew. This threw too much weight on the other dual and it, a little worn, went also. Have you ever replaced tires at a "Last Chance Before Vegas" tire shop in the desert, or paid for a seventy-five-mile tow? Not fixing that tire till later cost over $500!

Likewise, a friend of mine had a butane tank with a leak—a tiny, tiny leak that he was going to fix later. Later was (as usual) longer than he thought, and when fixing time forced itself upon him, the barbecue dinner was only half done and the butane had all leaked out. Now what would have only involved a fifty-cent washer was a hurried trip to the store, $19 worth of butane lost, and picnic-ful of hungry people.

High producers learn to fix things not only when it's time to do so, but early. They don't wait for something to make them fix it at the worst possible moment. You're going to have to deal with broken or nonworking things sometime, for sure, so why not *now*, while they're in your control? That's what the go-getters do.

To summarize and remind us of the power of early, I've included a couple of charts here.

More Magic of Early			
Daily Detail	**Late**	**On Time**	**Early**
Lines	Stand and wait.	Stand in a shorter line.	No line!
Parking	Walk six blocks/ pay a lot.	Fight other on-timers for the last two spots.	Get the closest spot and back your car in.
A visit	No time left so just wave.	A little "get-together."	A chance to really touch base.
A bargain	No bargaining power.	Average deal.	A real bargain.
Cleaning	Have to let it go.	Time to wipe.	Time for those extra little touches.
Choice of	Leftovers.	Already picked over by the early birds.	First choice.
Pit stop	Cross your legs and hold it.	60 percent chance.	Take any stall for as long as you want.
Seat	Fight—search—steal.	Take what they point you toward.	Choose where you want to sit.
Travel	Sweat and hurry.	Accomplish your objective.	Do a half-dozen little extras on the way.
Emergency	Worsens stress, risks, and problems.	Anxiety, risks, and problems.	You are calmer and in a better position to solve the problem.
Menu	Others have already ordered for you.	Quick read and decision.	Thoughtful selection and delightful meal.
Weather	It has the upper hand.	It dampens the situation.	You have time to take steps to counteract it.

More Magic of Early			
Daily Detail	**Late**	**On Time**	**Early**
Traffic	Use the horn.	Go slower.	No problem!
Anxiety	Intensified.	Normal amount.	Less or none.
Paperwork	Increases.	Remains a drag.	Reduced.
Report or other assignment	Lower grade, even if the paper is excellent.	Meets the requirements.	Time to pursue new thoughts or leads, no deadline stress.
Injury or medical problem	Prolonged pain, possible infection or permanent damage.	Stop or reduce pain and damage.	Prevent pain and damage.
A bill	Dunning calls and letters, interest charges and penalties.	Meet obligation.	Improve credit rating, impress others, possibly get discount.
Pest control	Problem insect/ bird/animal multiplies and does lots of damage.	Stop damage and annoyance.	Prevent damage and annoyance.
Hiring	Whomever is at hand.	The best of who's available now.	Time to find *the* best.
Time exchange rate	Ten minutes late takes one hour from you.	Even exchange.	Ten minutes ahead gains you an hour.

What do you want to say with your life? Just about all of your plans and projects, and ultimately your reputation, will be affected if not controlled by which column you choose here. As you can see, I believe that even "on time" is late.

Your Timing Talks for You

LATE says . . .	ON TIME says . . .	EARLY says . . .
I'm not interested.	Okay—as expected (yawn).	I'm really interested.
I'm not ready.	Okay—as expected (yawn).	I'm ready.
I'm behind.	Okay—as expected (yawn).	I'm ahead.
I'm uncomfortable.	Okay—as expected (yawn).	I'm comfortable.
I have no confidence.	Okay—as expected (yawn).	I'm confident.
I'm desperate.	Okay—as expected (yawn).	I'm relaxed.
I'm out of control.	Okay—as expected (yawn).	I'm in control.
I'm leaving a lot to chance.	Okay—as expected (yawn).	I have a choice.
I'll take whatever's left.	Okay—as expected (yawn).	I get what I want.
I don't care about others.	Okay—as expected (yawn).	I care about your feelings.
I'm buried.	Okay—as expected (yawn).	I'm on top of things.
I'm a taker.	Okay—as expected (yawn).	I'm a giver.
I'm preoccupied.	Okay—as expected (yawn).	I'm available.
I can't make deadlines.	Okay—as expected (yawn).	I don't need deadlines.
My style is "crisis management."	Okay—as expected (yawn).	I plan ahead.
I don't look beyond the moment.	Okay—as expected (yawn).	I look ahead.
I'm a follower.	Okay—as expected (yawn).	I'm a leader.
I have to be coerced.	Okay—as expected (yawn).	I can do it on my own.
People snarl at me.	Okay—as expected (yawn).	People smile at me.
This costs.	Okay—as expected (yawn).	This pays.
Poor.	*Average.*	*Excellent.*

FINALLY, you get to pick your label to live by. Be sure to pick one you'll be content to live with the rest of your life.

The Great Transformation Day

Lots of full-grown folks still believe in the fairy godmother who, one of these days, will grant a magical change in personal production. If we've attended enough training sessions, heard and memorized all the virtues of industriousness, one day (zap!) we will cross the line from poky to productive. It's a fairy tale. The skills of exceptional production are gradually attained, not instantly ordained.

So don't get discouraged if you aren't seeing any magnificent transformations. The only change of habit or behavior that might yield anything immediately is changing over to being *early* in everything. The results of that particular transformation are pretty astounding. The rest of a high producer's habits take practice and a while to ingrain before they can guarantee you time blessings.

Chapter 6
How about Some Help?

Seems like many of the super-doers we admire have all the luck and talent, or like they were born with a silver stopwatch in their pockets. That's absolutely not true! What is true is that they get more than their share of help and assistance.

High producers aren't lone wolves or one-man shows, as you might first imagine. In fact, they are the best team-workers around. They need and get all the help they can, all the time. And their sources of it are simple and available to anybody.

Before sharing some of these aids of the high achievers, let's take a look at some "helps" that aren't such a big help.

Forget about "the Big Break"

We always hear about that one great record-breaking feat, master move on the market, or "Hail Mary" pass, etc.—where a single event made a name or millions for someone. This is often referred to as "the big break." Lottery winners, software geniuses, or racecar drivers are suddenly "somebody" because they did something newsworthy. People hear this so much that they end up waiting for the big moment or break that will make them. That's why so many people end up disappointed with their lives. Never mentioned in the headlines are the rest of the facts:

1. The lottery player spent $10,000 on tickets before she won that million, and 14 million other lottery players got nothing that day.
2. The software genius worked out of his garage for fifteen years as he built his business, eating nothing but tuna and canned soup.
3. The race car driver lost 167 races, was burned over thirty percent of his body once, and his passion for racing has cost him two marriages so far.

Don't be deceived by "big breaks"; they seldom come.

Whatever you do, don't waste your precious time and emotions gambling and praying and waiting for a big magical event triggered by someone (or something) else to put you on top. Don't live for the big light that is going to come on some day to make you rich, famous, secure, productive, and happy forever. That will only happen if you pick up many little sticks for a long time and build a bright fire. Most accomplishments are the results of many small things added up over time. Don't save yourself for the spectacular, for the headlines. Score soundly in every game instead of dreaming of that one "forty point" night. Production always has a history, and *consistency* is what counts.

Forget about "the Ledge"

Another big time-waster is the search for the elusive "ledge." Once we set out on life's road we only pick up speed, rules, responsibilities, opportunities, dreams—and more and more to do. Sooner or later this pressure begins to get to us, and this is when the idea of the "ledge" is formulated. Somewhere ahead there will be a ledge, a sanctuary, a rest stop, where we can leap out of the stream or jump off the merry-go-round. Time will stop there, and noises and demands too, and we will be able to just lie there for a while and recover. After we've nursed our road wounds and calmly collected ourselves, we can do all that letter writing and meditation, complete all those undone chores and waiting projects. Then, all restored and rested, we can leap off the ledge and back into the fight of life, much the better now with no backaches or backlog.

Everyone has their dream of the ledge. Maybe it would be a minor injury to put you harmlessly out of commission for a while so you have time to catch up as you convalesce. Maybe it's a vacation, or maybe you dream of being snowbound for a week. You just need that little ledge—that release from the rat race—to stop and service, to fix, heal, and refuel.

Most of us are still looking and waiting for that ledge. We want salvation from society's demands and our crazy schedules and all those commitments before they drive us insane or work us to death. There isn't a single one of us who hasn't been on the watch for the ledge. In fact, we anticipate it with a great list of the things we are going to get done when we finally reach it.

I had been looking for my ledge since the age of twenty-one, and in my fifties I finally realized that there ain't one! And anything I thought was a ledge, wasn't—it was just a shoulder on the road loaded with more to do.

"Stopping to catch up" is, unfortunately, an idle wish. How many of us ever get time to stop? With each passing year it only gets harder to find any time to stop and catch up. And even if you can manage to stop the clock, it probably won't aid your productivity. Most of the time when people do stop to catch up, they're so relieved to be stopped, they fall further behind.

The bottom line is, you are going to have to stay on the road and fix yourself out in the open of the fast lane. You don't get to stop to get more done; you have to do it on the run, and you can.

You Can't Run Long on Starter Fluid (Motivators)

On those far-below-zero mornings on the Idaho ranch where I grew up, it was hard to get going in the morning, and even harder to get the big tractors to go. Those cold engines often didn't have enough oomph to turn over. We couldn't risk the chance that they might not run, or that we'd run the battery down trying to get them started, so we had a fantastic little can of stuff called "starter fluid." A tiny bit of that sprayed onto the air filter would be sucked into the piston chamber area and turn even a flicker of a spark into a running engine. Dad would always caution us, "Not too much, just a bit, these engines can't run on starter fluid. Once they fire, the regular gas will take over." Once the engine was warm it then started easily anytime during the day.

All of us who constantly seek a "motivator" to keep us going could take a lesson from this. You can't run long on motivators—stimulants, prizes, and other outside incentives—for accomplishment. A motivator is sometimes necessary to assure survival and progress, but if it continues too long it will cause weakness and damage. A motivator should only be used like Dad recommended for the starter fluid—"just a tiny bit." You can't run on motivators. If you did, you'd need constant fixes. And you'd fold when the motivators ran out because, like starter fluid, motivators are expensive. Motivators simply help produce a spark that *may* turn into the powerful continuous strokes of work.

Motivators may rouse us to accomplishment, but accomplishment is the sustaining reality. Once you build and produce, once your work results in something that changes a life, a structure, a direction, then you'll be changed, too, and your accomplishment will feed you just like a tank of fuel feeds a big engine.

Delegation Won't Do It All for You, Either

Is delegating responsibilities and tasks to others a sure ticket to higher productivity, as so many seminar leaders tell us? A more cynical definition of this oversold "magic principle" of time management might be this:

> **Delegation: An act that gives you the comforting illusion that something is being taken care of, until you have time to deal with it yourself.**

Delegation can be a way of doing more and better if:

- You can afford to hire someone to help.
- The delegate is competent and responsible.
- The delegate is motivated and punctual.
- The delegate understands, clearly and completely, what you want him or her to do.

These qualifications eliminate a goodly number of the people you might delegate anything to. Delegation isn't an instant way out of management responsibility, nor is it the cure-all solution it's constantly claimed to be. Half the stuff we're told to delegate, we could and should do ourselves. You can delegate a duty or task, but not the motivation and commitment to do it. You can delegate authority, but not your own accountability for how things turn out. You need to be able to distinguish between things that can be delegated or intelligently assigned, and things that you should take care of yourself.

Some delegating can easily take longer than doing it your-self, by the time you choose someone to delegate to, explain it all to the person, try to get him or her invested in it, and then check up to evaluate and keep quality control on what the person is doing . . . and repair mistakes. **It doesn't make much sense to delegate out work that you can do yourself.** and then spend days following up on the delegate's work—unless you're planning to work with him or her regularly.

I was once a volunteer supervisor of six buildings in six neighboring communities. My work involved overseeing the cleaning of the buildings, ordering cleaning materials and equipment; hiring, training, and supervising the custodians and determining their salaries; ordering fuel to heat the build-ings; and doing repairs, painting, etc., as needed. And then I had to submit reports on it all. This appeared to be a big job, and I was empowered to employ assistants, committees, order clerks, and other "people power" to make the job easier. I did the job by myself for four years, and did it well. It took about three hours a week at the most, never derailed my schedule, and was really enjoyable. When a custodian wanted some-thing, I made myself available and talked it over with him or her for a few minutes, then took another five to personally write out the order and mail it. I had the product sent to me, and when I passed one of the buildings I'd drop it off, visit with the staff, and inspect the building, working it in with other activities. I always knew exactly what was going on, and was able to make my monthly reports in minutes.

The person who replaced me followed the organization's procedure manual and lined up assistants, helpers, and order-getters, complicating the job by at least ten times. When someone would call for an order, my replacement would take it, and then call the order person, who would then order it. The product would be shipped to the building, and no one ever knew when (or if) it came in, so the custodian had to make an inquiry into it, or call the order clerk to run it down.

The order clerk would then hunt down and call the custodian; he would call her back, and so on and on down the "chain of command." When the monthly report had to be done, the whole process was even more complicated, and just locating and finding out things and calling people took a lot of time. Administrating took so much time, there wasn't time left to train, supervise, or clean! The job consumed thirty hours a week and my replacement hated it!

Too many people given leadership and management jobs think the whole idea is to get someone else to do all the work, including a professional assistant to hand out assignments. But a highly paid management job or the running of a team or home aren't delegation jobs, they are working, making-it-work jobs, where you do all you can toward achieving the goal, and only assign those things it wouldn't be smart for you to do, or that others can do more quickly and efficiently than you.

The fastest way to slow down productivity is to remove yourself from the scene, from experiencing and facing and being part of what's going on. Being reported to, rather than being part of the report, will wean you from the real world fast, and ultimately you'll pay for it with time!

Taking Tools to Task

Tools are cool! Tools are the very essence of human accomplishment, our claim to fame in history—their value is almost incalculable. Any one of us without our tools is generally slow and unproductive, if not helpless.

We certainly can enhance our ability to produce by finding and using the right tools. Farmers found tending the fields hard labor indeed until they invented tools to assist them. Surgeons saved more lives as their tools evolved beyond the simple knife or the scalpel. Food preparation is certainly faster and easier with the right utensils. You can catch more fish with the

right tackle. So the old expression "Get a bigger hammer" does have merit when it comes to accomplishing many things.

But we must never forget that tools are tools—implements, utensils, gear. They don't perform—we do.

Confusing the task with the tool is bad news because nothing ruins a good person faster than getting in the habit of letting failure or success always be the result of a tool. Take, for example, the common cop-out "My computer's down." That's like announcing the end of the world, the cessation of life as we know it—"offline." In other words, the tool is broken, so time stops. We, not our tools, make things happen.

New trucks (terrific tools) don't help a floundering trucking company if the drivers don't show up for work or can't read a map. When you're mining, a hydraulic two-story dredge sure is faster and better than a gold pan, but it doesn't matter how much faster and better if you don't find gold. A wise and well-trained mechanic will benefit from new tools. A poor mechanic won't make an engine run any better with the best wrenches money can buy. A surgeon who arrives late won't save the life, even with the most modern tools medicine can provide. The Little Leaguer who misses batting practice won't hit home runs just because his dad bought him a $70 bat.

Tools don't hit and tools don't score! Tools don't accomplish, either. Tools are only instruments.

Something as insignificant as a lunch bag can make a big difference in your life. By using it to avoid going "out" to eat (solving the problems of interruptions, poor diet, and how to achieve better use of your time) you can have 300 extra hours a year, 3,000 in ten years, 18,000 hours or more than two years of free time in a lifetime—all from a tool! Just remember that the lunch bag didn't do it, your use of it did!

Likewise, hardware, closet, or stationery organizers don't actually organize, they're just tools to use. They won't do any sorting on their own, and they won't put anything back or away by themselves.

More errors of judgment are made when machines are involved than anywhere on the purely human side of productivity. If there's a chance that a machine is going to take away some of the work and make the job faster, then we back off and somehow think the machine is going to do it all. Machines don't do the work, and they're not responsible, they're just an extension of us—we still have to plan, direct, and enact.

The computer is a great tool, but it isn't an all-knowing, all-doing, self-operating manager—it's just a better shovel. "It can *do* so many marvelous things," people say. Not so. It doesn't *do* them—it helps *you* do them.

|||||||||||||||||||||||||||||||||||||||||||||||||||||||||||||||||||||||||||||||||||||||||||

Ahhh—the computer, a proven wonder tool to enhance production! The plow, in its day, was of equal value, but not much use without ground to plow. Worthwhile material to feed a computer is like that tillable ground. It's got to be there or the tool is useless.

|||||||||||||||||||||||||||||||||||||||||||||||||||||||||||||||||||||||||||||||||||||||||||

All of my books, which have sold more than 3 million copies, were originally typed on a 1959 Olympia manual typewriter I bought for $5. This is what the world's most prolific writer, James Michener, used, too—an old manual typewriter (without a spelling corrector, mind you!).

I own hundreds of computers now through my various companies, and I'm amazed at what they can help us do, as well as how easily they can actually interfere with production when they aren't used intelligently.

You have to be careful here—many of the tools designed to help us do things faster and better, if we're not in control of them, will end up hurting how much we get done. I remember the first time I used an airless spray gun, for example. That thing was really impressive. It shot out a perfectly even three-foot spread of paint, and kept one guy busy full time just keeping it fed. It saved so much time that five painters all stood around and watched it in awe. So even though I had a tool capable of speeding up the work, more work didn't get done that day. That job ending up taking six people!

Advanced Communications Equipment

A business associate and I were eating lunch at a fried chicken place not long ago, and a fellow strutted in carrying a cell phone. While downing two drumsticks, a plate of wings, and a great mound of coleslaw, he took three calls and made two more, all trivial, all the while talking in a booming voice to inform the whole restaurant of how important he was.

I haven't noticed many high producers weighted down with advanced communications equipment—but the rookies sure love it. They don't seem to realize that no matter how quickly or ingeniously contact is made, the reason for the call still has to be dealt with. And maybe it should have been done before you got on the road or left home or town. There are some jobs for which instant contact—anywhere—is essential, but for many of us cell phones and all of their relatives are just one more distraction.

What a great tool a fax machine is, likewise, but it isn't a cure for ineptness or inability to get things done on time. It's a tool for quicker turnaround of printed communication.

Fast tools actually hurt poor managers because such tools give them the impression that they're managing, when they're just catching up.

||||||||||||||||||||||||||||||||||||||||||||||||||||||||||||||||||||||||||||||||

Answering machines were wrongly named. They aren't answering machines, they're question collectors. YOU have to, at some later and perhaps even more inconvenient time, do the answering (or ignoring). Most of the things on them could have been handled faster, better (and cheaper) with early mail.

||||||||||||||||||||||||||||||||||||||||||||||||||||||||||||||||||||||||||||||||

Bigger and Better Machines May Not Be the Answer

You might be surprised how much can still be done most efficiently "by hand." One day, for instance, we had three post holes to dig on the corral at my ranch. My son said, "Let's use the automatic post-hole digger, Dad, it can dig a hole a minute." I told him each hole would only take ten minutes by hand. "But that's thirty minutes of work," he said.

"Yes, but it's faster than the hour it will take to put the digger on the tractor, and then take it off again, so we'll save at least a half hour doing it by hand," I replied.

You don't always need a new or bigger machine to do more. Sometimes phoning for, waiting for, getting, and directing a machine takes longer and costs considerably more.

Another time, a gravel hauler showed up at my place and dumped the twelve cubic yards of gravel I ordered in the middle of the road. He asked me where I was going to get a loader or tractor to spread it out. Then he left for another load and returned in forty-five minutes. When he returned, the entire load was spread neatly around, and there was no heavy machinery in sight. Living on and around such equipment all his life, the guy never realized what a single person can do by hand with just a shovel and wheelbarrow.

Before we got a manure loader on the front end of the tractor, my Dad used to move twelve loads of manure a day, filling one of those big old spreaders full each time by hand, with a pitchfork. He got the job done and was super-productive. The new rig could do it faster, but it was expensive, and 95 percent of the year it just sat there, and it required a lot of work to maintain. That maintenance often took more time than the hand work did!

People do this with equipment all the time. Haul in a $175 backhoe to dig a one-hour, $10 hole—because the machine is the latest way to do it! (Then, go to the gym and pay to get some physical exercise.)

How many farmers have gone under after buying ever bigger and better machinery, convinced that it would compensate for production lags or price sags? On the ranch where I grew up we had a little Allis Chalmers all-crop harvest combine worth about $1,500 that cut five-foot swaths. It took us a week longer to cut our grain with it than the neighbors, who bought equipment that made twelve-foot cuts. They finished up their harvest in two days, and then that $30,000 investment sat the other 363 days—a poor and deadly use of tools.

In my own line of work I run across millions of people who, in an effort to make cleaning easier, over-tool. Under their sinks, in their cleaning closets and pantries, are arsenals of cleaning potions and paraphernalia that would service the

Empire State Building for a month. Yet the house is a mess. More and better tools aren't the answer to everything. Over-tooling can easily kill initiative rather than give us more time and ease.

Bigger and better machines don't always buy us time, even if logically, in theory, and on paper they're ten times faster than by hand. So be careful when it comes to automating yourself. Automation works well and is productive in a factory because factories do the same thing over and over again—you seldom do. You're a producer, not a production line, and that's a big difference!

Bigger, better, newer, faster, more accurate tools are all time-use plusses for you as long as you don't depend on them to do your work, or end up in their hands instead of they in yours. Think! A little logic will keep you the taskmaster. An engineer friend pointed out to me one day, for example, as he watched me spade the whole garden in one hour with my shovel: "Don, if you doubled the size of your shovel, you'd do it in a half hour." As technically and mathematically correct as he might be, I'd have a hard time lifting the load on that bigger shovel over and over, so the job might take three days (or forever) with a bigger and better tool.

Let's move on to the real helpers now, and start with the best one—

Look to Your Fellow Man or Woman (Volunteers!)

How do you get them to help? Well, you put up a sign that says:

- I Am a Nice Person
- I Need/Want Help
- It Is Going to Be Fun . . .
- And You Can Be Part of It!

Yes, most super-doers have a sign exactly like this and they wear it twenty-four hours a day. Haven't you seen the sign on them? It is there and the reason it works so well is because everyone else sees it too.

This is how go-getters manage to recruit so much help. They make their paths public. They aren't bashful about telling the world what they are up to: "This is what I'm going to do, and when and how and why." The average person is cautious and even terrified about publicly charting the future (in case something goes wrong). High producers get people to lead for them, not just follow, by selling ahead.

We all have an immediate attraction to well-directed people. We join with them in spirit and build a loyalty to them without even realizing it. This is because doers have a definite direction, a destination. They are going somewhere, moving, and any progress or action is exciting. The average person has been waiting for something like this and is grateful for it, so he or she willingly and enthusiastically contributes to the task at hand. People love to be busy—they want in on, to be part of, "important goings-on."

This help from fellow humans is perhaps the most precious resource you will ever deal with, because it involves other people's lives and time. The doers who get the most help are usually unselfish. They don't hog all the fun and glory. So make sure your own sharing is regular and generous. Share credit for accomplishments, praise, and profits.

Personal Counsel (the Free Kind)

There are a lot of good, knowledgeable people out there and, surprising as it may be, they are among the most willing and generous when it comes to sharing what they know. These people are my favorite sources of information, evaluation, and instruction.

Some people are a little critical of "follow the leader" for life lessons, so they end up following the followers instead. When you're looking for advice, pick a real performer; by no means does this have to be a "professional" (who charges) or a professor. If someone checks out, is genuinely productive, proven, and exemplary, what better pattern and pal would you want? Daily, I seek out and get advice from others whose watch has a different face and ticks differently than mine. Some are women, some men, some young, some old, some only eighth-grade graduates, but they are all experts and they like to be asked. A fourteen-year-old into bikes or beekeeping can give you more solid direction, answers, opinions, and demos in an hour of one-on-one than most books or courses could in days or weeks. I've done a number of successful real estate deals, although I know little about the subject. What's my secret? Before I act, I talk to my friends who have been successful in real estate and ask questions. I get excellent input on a variety of subjects from many of those who work for me, be they managers or minimum-wage crewmembers.

Once I identify my expert, I visit with him or her for a little while till I learn what I need to deal with my problem or do what I have in mind. The person who not only has blazed a trail somewhere you want to go, but has gone on to build a highway out of that trail is an especially good source to tap.

The Hang-Around Law

Big doers are always busy, but don't let that deter you. If you can't get to them right off, then just apply what I call the Hang-Around Law. There are some super-producers in the world who know how and why and what to do, and just being around them will teach you more in days than you can learn in years from a theory-rehasher. They aren't all working for big companies, either—some of the best producers are running little restaurants or stores right in your town or city somewhere.

I tried forever, for example, to learn to play the guitar. I read books and plinked and plunked and after two years could play "Twinkle, Twinkle Little Star" (partly). Then, a good guitar player moved in across the street and a couple of times a week I lugged my instrument over there. I hung around and listened and asked, and learned more in two weeks than in the whole two years previous.

> Contact, watch, and work with brilliant doers.
> Pay attention to how they get ready, aim, and
> fire. And notice when their house lights come
> on in the morning and go off at night.

If you really want to learn how to accomplish, find a successful working mother and follow her around and watch her for a few days. It will beat any college course in Dynamic Doing 101. She wakes up with a full load and gains forty unexpected add-ons and emergencies over the course of the day—and have you ever seen a break time for that mother? Watch how she does it, by determination and instinct, plus a strong survival drive, fueled by love and genuine concern for her family. She never stops or slows down and somehow it all gets done.

So hang around the masters and observe and ask, even work for them for a while. You'll absorb habits and techniques that will serve you well. You can learn more by watching than by being lectured. Go-getting is easy to show and hard to tell.

Group Helpers

Handling individual helpers is not too hard or risky, but having groups come to your aid can be a genuine two-edged sword when it comes to time-cutting.

There are at least four sources of collective aid for your projects and undertakings:

1. Committees
2. Meetings
3. Seminars and courses
4. Associations

All of these can be lifesavers, but if you're not careful they can drain the life out of your project—and use up your time.

Committees

Some marvelous works have come from committees—great relationships have been built, new leaders have been identified and tested, scattered brilliance has been pooled into blockbuster accomplishments.

On the other hand, the notes, records, and plaques that record and reward each member after committee meetings and proceedings could fill 500 Libraries of Congress.

The key to a committee's accomplishment, regardless of the array of talent, is usually its *leader*. In many cases, a committee of five works best when four don't show up and the leader just gets the job done. Granted, many committees do end up with some kind of a result, but that result seldom justifies the great expenditure of time involved—all the travel and refreshments, and all the explanations and reporting. When you find yourself on a committee that is being organized for something, do the work all yourself the night before and donate the expenses. You'll be time and money ahead.

Meetings

Notice in brochures, ads, movies, and TV shows how the big-time action so often takes place in a "meeting." The big boss is at the head of a table conducting a meeting. The ad people are assessing the latest advertising campaign for No Sweat deodorant in a meeting.

|||||||||||||||||||||||||||||||||||||||||||||||||||||||||||||||||||

**Meetings: When all is said and done,
more is always said than done.**

|||||||||||||||||||||||||||||||||||||||||||||||||||||||||||||||||||

People run things from conference tables in meetings. Not only executives but parents, teachers, and preachers make their power moves in meetings, and crooks even plan their next big heists in meetings. Thus we are primed and persuaded that the best way to handle anything is to "hold a meeting."

This is probably one of the biggest management myths going. Meetings only have a few truly worthwhile purposes, such as to inform or teach a group, or to exchange thoughts on a problem. But even for these purposes, assembly is not the only or always the best means to an end. At least 80 percent of meetings are too long or unnecessary, and they bog down our ability to accomplish instead of helping it. A group converging on a problem doesn't guarantee anything. Parleys don't assure production. When people sit down too long or too often to talk, trouble is always on the agenda.

In business or at home, I've found that most people already know before a "meeting" what they've done or haven't done, and what they should do. The main purpose the meeting serves is to discuss the excuses or distribute the blame.

Actual work can rarely be done in a meeting—planning or divvying it up, maybe, or gathering ideas for it, but no actual work. Somewhere, sometime, somebody has to go out and do the job.

Isn't it amazing how when we call or visit to get something done, even when it's essential that we get ahold of someone, we buy the line "Oh she's in a meeting." It's like meetings are sacred, immune to everyday necessities. **The job–getting it done–is the only sacred entity to a go-getter.** A meeting is just an appendage of production, so real action shouldn't be interrupted for a meeting.

Next time you call a meeting, watch how much time everyone uses up fitting the meeting in instead of taking care of the problem the meeting is being called for. Can you imagine a mother or father of eight holding a meeting for every crisis and need in household management?

What would happen if, just before you walked into a meeting (just like when you go to a movie or concert), you had to pay what the meeting really cost, in both your life's time and cold cash? You'd want to roll on the floor and kick and groan. Totally worthless "intra-office" business meetings, for example, can easily cost $1,000 or more in wages and snacks—and big fly-in meetings, $100,000 or more. Often, this is all for a discussion or assignment that could be accomplished by phone or in an e-mail exchange, or by someone doing the job right the first time.

"We've got to talk." Fine, do it, but don't make it a formal meeting with bagels, coffee, and juice. When someone says,

"Let's meet on it," you don't always need a conference room, an opening and closing speech, handouts, and refreshments!

|||||||||||||||||||||||||||||||||||||||||||||||||||||||||||||||||||||||||

Participate fully in the meetings that really matter, or where your particular expertise is essential. Whenever possible, wiggle out of, or send someone else to, all the rest.

|||||||||||||||||||||||||||||||||||||||||||||||||||||||||||||||||||||||||

The more I avoid meetings of any kind, the faster and more effective I get. It's amazing how much less essential a meeting becomes when I say, "Sure, we can have a meeting. How about 6:00 A.M.? I have some time then." I get dead silence from salespeople and business associates after that, and they finally stutter and say, "Well, you know, Don, I could just send the material to you."

Starting today, just for the fun of it, keep track of the actual production result or gain from meetings. You'll find so little you'll be surprised, and soon you won't find yourself in so many meetings.

Seminars (and Related Rah-Rah Courses)

There are, in any group of professional "instructors," giants of wisdom and master teachers. There are also sincere but uninspired presenters, as well as parrots—people who are simply collectors and presenters of good production mottoes and stories and philosophy. And still further down (getting the biggest fee), there are glittering, media-made celebrities, good-looking folks whose credentials for teaching finance, family management, or how to get more done are question-able but seldom questioned.

I speak with some expertise here, since I'm among the pla-toons of productivity experts roaming campuses, convention halls, clubs, and companies, and appearing in commercials. I've taught thousands of seminars, attended hundreds of them, and financed tens of thousands of dollars' worth of them for my employees to attend.

Seminars range from life-changing to totally useless. We've all known plenty of people who took courses and seminars and were no better when they came out than when they went in. About all they gain is a little arm strength from carrying huge binders of rules and principles back and forth from the classroom. Among the thousands of well-sold seminars out there (from getting rich in real estate to getting a date, from saving your lawn to saving your marriage) running $49.95 to $1,400 (plus expenses, recordings, etc.), a few are a solid help. Many more will just pour molasses in your clock. Selecting according to your direction is the first step in thinning down the choices. **Pay attention to who is teaching you.** Impressive titles and trendy theories don't guarantee worth; in fact, you at times may have more go-getter and producing wisdom than the person you're seeking out as a teacher.

"Behaviorist," "expert," "Ivy League graduate," "former member of the president's staff," "advisor," "manager," "doctor of . . . ," "noted," "celebrated," "certified," "sought after" can all be so much horse manure. *Who* is the teacher, and is he or she a real doer or simply a researcher and collector of other doers' deeds? If he or she IS a master of the thing you're eager to learn, will you get the master, or a staff member who memorizes a presentation and dishes it out to you for $495 a day? I hate to hand my executives, my children, or myself over to mere polish or piles of projected analysis of "never happened." Check the leader out—anyone can write a book, be on TV, or get a degree these days. This doesn't necessarily qualify a person to stand at the head of hundreds and sound off. If he or she personally exemplifies where you want to be—pack up and attend!

Associations, Memberships, Organizations

Bus drivers, teachers, janitors, farmers, pilots, chemists, car restorers, well drillers: Just about every profession, hobby, and career has an organization or association. We all belong to some, and I've spoken to or taught hundreds of them.

The purpose of most organizations is good and pure. Uniting to pool resources is a great idea, as is having an official place and time to exchange information, upgrade, and inspire each other. Well chosen and used, groups and associations can help you improve your productivity and enhance the growth and quality of any direction or undertaking.

True to usual form, however, we humans can and do quickly clutter up and complicate purity. Before you know it, those members are getting together not just to exchange wisdom but to socialize and add members. And then, logically, there are dues—and, of course, anything structured needs administration, officers, some kind of government, and a system to distribute material/mail.

Far too many of the once-beneficial associations we belong to have become self-serving, thus self-consuming. They spend most of their peoplepower and money organizing the organization rather than advancing the goals. Here's an example you're probably familiar with. I receive magazines, newsletters, and reports from a nationally known association. One of those reports arrived not long ago, and only one page of the entire publication was information to help the members of the association. The rest of the "report" concentrated on:

1. Personality and travel of officers
2. Election of officers—lists and pictures of candidates
3. Evaluation of the past, present, and future of the organization
4. Activities at board meetings
5. Awards for achievements of officers
6. The President's report (overly personal and poorly done)

7. Thank-yous for awards and notes
8. Pages of pictures of people standing with cocktail glasses in their hands
9. Membership drive graphs/reports
10. Plagiarized poems
11. Survey questionnaires about the association

If we pulled many an association's reports, we would see pages and pages clearly revealing the focus as more on entertainment than education or edification. The same is true of potentially valuable conferences and conventions. "I have to search for a class or session out of twenty going on to find one that actually helps me!" is a common complaint from someone spending four or five days at expensive association convention spots. Here again, there may be a worthwhile purpose and some potential help from attending the conference, but it's a risky expenditure of time. Watch for and consider the unquestionably enhancing organizations and courses; the rest you probably want to avoid on the road to becoming a high producer.

How to Get More Done with Others

The real producer doesn't simply turn things over to others or join up with others to accomplish a task. The doer steers the boat and maintains control. How you go about the "multi-person" type of project can make a tremendous difference in output and accomplishment. Let's say, for example, you have to meet with another person to discuss a project you will be undertaking together. There are three possible outcomes of the first meeting:

1. If you meet or begin the project and neither of you is ready, committed, or organized, and neither of you has done much preparation and planning, you'll probably get only a dozen worthwhile work-related exchanges made.

2. If you meet and YOU really have the thing organized on your side—direction set, ideas and outlines written up, samples ready, sketches done, or whatever—and the other person is still totally unprepared, you'll still get almost double the amount of things done, compared to the first possibility.

3. If you meet and both of you are 100 percent clued in, organized, and prepared, you will achieve the ultimate of useful transactions, almost three times as many as the first scenario.

This is such a simple secret to getting more done with others, but it took me years to wake up to it. I'd always catch people at random, without warning, to get something done or going. Gradually, I learned that when I dealt with other people, if I thought our task over first, wrote my thoughts down, drew up some plans, etc., and came to the person with a possible solution (not just a question or a problem), I got twice as much done. Then, one day I realized that if I insisted on the same from all the people who came to *me,* I could get even more done, and it would be better and faster.

Just do this for the next few weeks with everyone, at home and work, when they want to deal with or go over something with you. Tell them what to bring with them and where to meet, and watch your production go up and the amount of time it takes go down!

Some Hidden Helpers

All high producers have their little arsenal of hidden helpers—things that aid efficiency. These may be very ordinary or quite different from "the norm," but they work wonders for the doers. Some are physical, and some are intangible. Following are a few of mine.

1. Peace with People

You need to be at peace with those around you—those close to you, especially your spouse or partner, family, and everyday companions—because disharmony is the king of time- and energy-consumers. Disharmony takes you nowhere. It keeps you constantly occupied—coping with it, preparing for it, defending yourself against it, recovering from it. Your life companion will be one of the most significant factors in your time usage, your immediate family next, your coworkers and friends after that—the public affects you very little in comparison. Peace is the most silent, but strongest, supporter of doing more.

2. The Underused Secret of Spares

I bet one "spare" day a year will end up saving a year of your life, and that's a good trade. By spare day I don't mean a day off or a day to do spare things, I'm talking about a day to line up and put in place some spares, some extras of the things you're most likely to suddenly have a desperate need for. What are some of these spares that could easily save $50 or fifty minutes of hunting and fuming?

Keys! We'd all have traded our souls sometime for just one ninety-nine-cent extra key. Pens! We've all done more than our share of digging and darting around to find one to capture a note, comment, or phone number. Bolts, nuts, and screws! Not having enough of these (at pennies each) has screwed up lots of our life's time. Basic tools such as pliers and screwdrivers, too, cost very little, and often make all the difference.

What about plain old bread and milk? If I had a dollar for all the times some member of my family has had to leap in the car and speed to the store to get milk because we were almost out, I could have bought a dairy by now.

And, oh yes, spare cash. Anyone can have spare cash, even the poorest person. Yet 90 percent of people, rich or poor, do not have any on hand for emergencies or special occasions. Think of the times when even a spare $5 would have shortened a project or gladdened the heart of a child selling cookies.

Think of all the *time* and emotion expended on such things.

Tomorrow or sooner, hold a spare day. Here is a little starter list of spares to put in place now, so the next time you're on a roll you won't have to stop and seek them out:

- Keys
- Spare cash
- Grocery staples
- Toilet paper
- Tissues
- Paper towels
- Batteries of all kinds
- Light bulbs
- Pens/pencils
- Paper
- Postage stamps
- Scotch tape
- Camera film or digital memory cards
- Ink cartridge(s)
- Diapers
- Pantyhose
- Pet food and litter
- Band-Aids
- Gasoline for lawn mower
- Flashlight
- Scissors
- Alarm clock
- Umbrella
- Shoelaces
- Basic tools such as screwdriver, pliers

- Wrapping paper and bows
- Birthday and other greeting cards
- Frozen or canned food for emergencies or surprise company

3. Deliberate Duplication

This takes the "spare" idea one step further. Often, the cost of duplicating often-used tools is minimal in dollars and space.

I know an elderly widow who accomplishes a lot and is always prepared for things, despite the fact that she has some physical handicaps now. One morning she explained to a group of us at church how she manages this. She needs a cane or crutches to get around, and she can't easily carry things or get to the things she needs. So, she leaves a duplicate set of the needed tools to do the things she does a lot, in all the places she's likely to need them—bedside, couch, table, sun porch, etc. Then, when she gets there she can just start reading or quilting or whatever. I learned a lot from her and now have four hammers, for instance. There's one in the house, one in my truck, one in the shop, and one to loan out to kids and community projects. When I need to hammer something, I am hammering instead of hunting for my tool for an hour only to discover that I lent it out to a neighbor last week.

4. Intelligence Gathering

Explore whether it's been done before! Most high producers not only know, but honor and respect history. Before launching, buying, planning, or paying anything, they will usually ask the simple question, "Has this been done before?" A little review then of when, how, and why allows them to become aware of the six mistakes the first doer made, so the high producer can cut a ton of time and trouble from the procedure. I know we all like to do our own thing, but taking a little time to check into other producers' projects and prowess can give you a leg up on the old clock or calendar.

5. Make Your Workplace Everyplace

High producers never have to look for work—they keep their capacity to work and all their doing power with them. They carry what they want to accomplish, and don't leave it on a desk, disk, or in a drawer somewhere. This provides that wonderful aid to production: *availability!* Face it, folks, we aren't sedentary. We are always on the go, every one of us— rich, poor, famous, anonymous, winners, and losers; even our children are always rushing from one event to another. We are always moving.

And the workplace has almost gotten too busy to work in, hasn't it? "On the go" means lots of new and different places, and lots of traveling. Time experts now tell us we average five or six years of life traveling. Too often, when the body is moving the brain isn't. Many of us visit or listen to CDs, etc., and that, to a degree, is productive use of travel time, but most things have to be *done,* not just listened to, talked about, and planned for. Some of the anti-workers in the world tell you to leave your "work" behind or at the office. Why? If it rewards you, pays you, educates, interests, teaches you or your children, or changes others' lives for the better . . . why leave it behind?

It's easy to use travel time effectively—just take and keep your frontlog with you at all times. Having all your ideas and some portable work with you anywhere—work, play, ball games, vacations, church, etc.—is perfect for catching the inspiration that floats by sometimes when your mind is at rest or on something entirely different.

You can tailor how you want to transport your work. I bring the biggest allowable carry-on-bag-sized briefcase with some yellow pads, pens, a camera, ear plugs, and a package or two of raisins, and I can write a bestseller or map company strategy 35,000 feet in the air, in a cab, on a fishing stream, in church, in bed, at the dinner table, in front of the TV, on the tractor, in the hospital, at a TV station, or on the beach. The fun begins when your workplace is everyplace!

6. Time Fragments

We're always looking for big nuggets of time for doing, when the dust or fine grains of gold—saved, collected, and weighed—add up to the same or more. People have gotten rich just saving the gold dust splashed out into the carpets during weighing.

So it is with time. All of your blocks or big stretches of time may be spoken for, you may be busy then with other work or family duties, but what about in between—the time fragments? The time during commercials, riding to places, waiting, daydreaming. **Over-committing will teach you a lot about using time fragments.** How many of you have been tremendously busy, and felt you couldn't work another thing into your schedule if your life depended on it, and then a big extra job comes up, something you either need for survival or just love to do? You can't slack off your demanding schedule at home, on the job, or in the community, or hurry any of the things you already have to do. But when the week is over, you've also completed the extra job and it's well done. Everyone is amazed and asks how you did it, they ooh and aah. You think about it a minute (you really aren't extra-tired) and wonder yourself, "When and how *did* I do that?" You just used the time fragments, the timeouts, the breaks—the standing around, waiting, gossiping, and traveling times, and the forty other fragments of time that are available. They're always around and usually unused—those time fragments can bail you out.

> The great mistake is doing nothing at all because you
> could only do a little—enough littles add up to a lot.

Another reason to carry work with you is that you never know when and where dead time will occur. I get five or six letters written a day using time niches. And most of my proposals, promotion ideas, plans, and book manuscripts are done in tiny pockets of time on the go. In fact, the majority of the books I've written in recent years have all been done in the little spaces somewhere between my regular ten-hour working day, my family obligations, and my church jobs. And this is not a strain. It's a break, a relief, and a reward.

> Thoreau said it best: "What good is immortality,
> if we cannot use half an hour well here."

I watch Monday Night Football like some of you, and it always takes thirty minutes to play the last four minutes. That gives me twenty-six minutes to work, think, write, draw, and play with kids while the game is going on.

How many time niches do you have? Many janitors tell me they have six hours' worth of spare minutes during the working day. It's been estimated that the average American spends at least 2,000 hours a year just being a spectator or listener—that's almost a third of the entire year! We also spend at least thirty-six hours a year sitting in traffic. And still you say you have no time? Seize the moment and do something with it!

Spare minutes add up. Set a big bucket under a little drip, and when you come back in a few hours, the bucket is full. Impossible? Nope, just an example of the power of fragments.

A tiny stream of water can fill a large lake in no time! And even the biggest snowbank is made up of miniature snowflakes that fell down one by one.

7. You Don't Have to Do It in Person!

Another great timesaving skill is realizing that "in person" is by no means always necessary to accomplish things. There are a few times and occasions when we must be physically present for something, or when something serious might go wrong if we aren't. But you don't always have to appear to make an appearance.

We still seem to have that pioneer instinct to jump on our horse and go, but if you're out for greater productivity avoid this whenever possible. There is no such thing as a "quick trip to town," and going out doesn't just take time, gas, and energy. Seeing all those sights and people changes your mood and mode and it'll be hard to recapture the rhythm of solitary accomplishment when you return.

One of the most magic words here is "delivered." Once I used to go get or run down everything myself. Now I've learned that the little extra charge for room service, for example, saves getting yourself presentable enough to go down to the hotel dining room and eat (and probably having to wait another half hour or more after you get there, to get waited on). If what you need can't be delivered, see if anyone else who could make a quick stop and pick it up or take care of it for you is headed that way. Even many "must have your signature" things can be done for you by someone else via Power of Attorney.

I use the mail to run most of my errands, and prefer writing to making calls most of the time. Calling is better than going yourself, but there are some cautions here, too. One call usually expands into at least two more to check things out further, make sure you have the right person or department, etc. And phoned instructions usually require some written confirmation in the end anyway. So most messages, requests, and assignments I do in writing, and make a copy. Then it's done, clearly recorded, and understandable by all.

Checks and automatic deposits are another magic tool here, too. I know lots of people who run around for half a day after they get paid, paying bills and settling accounts and then boxing receipts. I run half a dozen businesses and several organizations and I haven't been inside a bank for years, not even once. They send things to be signed and I do the transactions sitting in one place for a few minutes. If your employer automatically deposits your paycheck on payday your check is usually immediately good for the full amount. You can even set up your account to automatically pay bills. Electronic and online banking and bill paying can save you literally days of work and effort.

Check, before you assume you must haul your body there!

8. Piggybacking

This happens naturally if you let it. While you're actively focusing on and doing one or two things, the answer, opportunity, or solution you need for several others will suddenly appear. Did those other problems or situations solve themselves? Not really. Your exposure to new skills, ideas, and sources in the course of the tasks you're doing now is what solved them.

This is how active and productive people seem to magically multiply their accomplishments. **Some things just happen while you're engaged in others,** and that is why you want to keep many projects and objectives with you at all times on your frontlog.

9. The Forgotten Workdays

There are fifty-two Saturdays and, counting all local, state, federal, and company holidays, about twenty other days a year to be off, to play, to celebrate, etc. You know—those "fun" days when most of the world is out killing each other on highways, crowding elbow to elbow in malls, fast-food stands, and bars, sitting in bumper-to-bumper traffic, and getting sunburned on beaches. By the time Saturdays and holidays draw to a close, most people have not only spent a lot of money, but they are exhausted, stressed, abused, and irritated. And they haven't actually had any fun, so they have to try again in the evening to squeeze out some enjoyment.

These "off days" are special and hold some big rewards for those willing to use them to do something that really counts in life. Working with and around the family, for example, gives us as much time together as driving through traffic, fighting crowds, and boating around an overcrowded lake with them. But boating is labeled "fun" and work is labeled "work," and so we avoid it, missing one of the best sources of personal pleasure. In fact, we probably have more meaningful contact and "one-on-one" time with someone raking the lawn or weeding the garden with him or her.

Before you get too caught up in that rhythmic little jingle "You deserve a break today," think for a minute of the opportunity to get things done when everyone *else* is out of the way taking a break! I find in business (and often at home too) that Saturdays and holidays are the best days to work and catch up and get ahead on things. While everyone else is out racing around or fighting lines and noise and congestion, in the office or your study at home there is peace and quiet and no crowding; the phone seldom rings, few visitors drop in, and you can really roll!

Working the off days built up my business, gave me a chance to be with the kids when they were out of school, and enabled me to get to know my employees better, fix up things around the house, help the neighbors, do church and community work, and even wash the windows! When the day was over, I'd tingle with satisfaction (and I'd saved money, energy, dignity, and personal injury, to boot!).

Today, Saturday work is almost a curse word; you hardly dare say it out loud—it's an insult, an imposition to even suggest it. But it's one of the hidden power secrets of the producers. Call it the Saturday sacrifice if you must, but try a new angle on fun—work some Saturdays. Get up early and start in on all the things you've been wanting to get done, those "somedays" that have been gnawing at you and that you've been getting nagged about. Do this for a couple of months and watch what happens, not only to your work, but to you, physically and mentally.

Talk about a high! Your Sundays and Mondays will immediately be better, and you'll laugh at all that play you used to pursue so passionately, because the rewards of the work done will be far superior!

As for holidays, many of us are less impressed than we used to be by them, anyway. We're a little more aware of the fact that these are the times we act silly and eat and drink and buy too much. It takes a real toll out of the paycheck as well as the time clock. Don't feel guilty about ignoring the holidays you care little or nothing about—it'll give you more time not only to accomplish but to celebrate the holidays you *do* really care about.

You can also reschedule your observation of a holiday or day off for greater efficiency. I still go fishing and go have fun, too, but not when the rest of the populace does. Fishing the day after an official holiday or on a Monday enables you to catch more big ones anyway because scores of fishermen haven't scared the fish off. And there's no traffic or crowds because everyone else is back to work or in deep recovery. Try working or staying home with the family on some of those holidays or "big event" days this year on a trial basis and you'll adopt the program forever.

‖‖‖

A productive vacation? Sure, vacations are made to get away or get reacquainted, to give us a change, to restore, refresh, and relax us. Playing dead for two weeks won't accomplish any of these. If you can make your work play or fit any of your accomplishment goals into the agenda, go ahead and do something productive during at least part of your vacation. Building something always beats extended idleness, and it's even more fun!

‖‖‖

10. Last and Most Important: Do Right

Follow the rules, obey the laws, and stay true to your ethics. Compare high and low producers and you'll find another parallel: righteousness and high production. Actually, it's only reasonable that those who do the right thing most of the time—tell the truth, treat others fairly, take good care of their bodies—are freer from encumbrances such as constantly having to cover up, dodge, repay, and cope with medical issues, fights, feuds, fines, and court appearances. Even the most talented potentially high producer can end up limiting himself or herself by traveling a crooked moral road. Trouble takes time and energy to undo, and then you have to harmonize yourself again with society.

If I had to pick the prime helper of all production, good old "Do what is right" would be number one on the list.

P.S. EARLY still gets you the most unsolicited help!

Chapter 7
Timepiece Tuners

This chapter offers some simple principles of greater effectiveness that will help you oil and fine-tune your accomplishment clock, and keep it running smoothly.

What Is the Objective?

We hear ourselves saying all too often after something is all over and it's too late, "Oh, *that's* what they wanted." By then we've lost more time than we'd like to admit to readying, bringing, or boning up on the wrong thing.

It took me years and some headaches and heartaches to learn to be sure I knew where the target was before I fired off my effort. Vague or too-general directions always create problems, and while we may somehow work our way through them to get the job done, it usually means lots of inefficiency, guesses, surprises, and delays. In my personal and business life I get thousands of calls and letters—requests for jobs, appearances, speeches, donations, help, information, and products. Eighty percent of them are unspecific, general requests. I finally learned to call or write back and say, "Tell me exactly what you want." If it's a speech they want me to make, I ask who is going to be attending, how many attendees there will be, who will speak before and after me, exactly what they would like my topic to be, and how long they want me to speak.

It's amazing how when that accurate and complete information finally arrives, you know whether you want to fill their request, and your job is half done.

Be Effective, Not Efficient

While gathering antiques for my cleaning museum, I came across a well-preserved seventy-year-old gadget with an enthusiastic "It works!" written under the price. It was identified as a "Screen Cleaner," and sure enough, I pushed it across a dusty screen and watched the little rollers, whiskers, and brushes operate perfectly, spinning, rolling, and humming with precise mechanics. But there was no way this thing would clean a screen that had—as so many of them do—embedded dirt, flyspecks, and grime. The Screen Cleaner didn't work—it operated. The manufacturer and seller confused movement with improvement.

How often, in pursuit of "doing," are we like that brush? We make motions and noise, turn gears, even raise some dust, but the earth's surface stays the same, as does our progress.

We can be efficient, cover a great deal of ground quickly, neatly, safely, economically, and even artfully, and still do little or nothing.

You can send a cowboy out into the hills on a roundup and he may be efficient and on time, ride perfectly, go fast and far, rope unerringly, know his steers and heifers, get saddle blisters on his butt, and sing all the campfire songs in tune. BUT if he doesn't bring back any cattle, it doesn't count.

You can rehearse and put on a stage play efficiently. But if it doesn't move the audience, inspire and change them or provide enjoyment, then it isn't effective.

I see lots of writers who have the tools and skills to turn out and organize copy, move paragraphs around perfectly and efficiently. But writing paragraphs that *move people* is the goal—and that's effectiveness. Efficiency is needed to be effective, but it's surely not an end in itself.

Concentrate Your Time Where It Counts

The secret of exceptional achievement lies in maximizing productive time and minimizing nonproductive time. I heard a lifeless talk once that clearly demonstrated what NOT to do here. The young speaker went to great lengths to describe why he'd been asked to talk, and how he'd prepared his speech. He then explained what he would talk about and how he would treat the subject. By this time, fifteen minutes of his allotted twenty-five were gone. He then sparsely covered his topic in five minutes. His clincher was a boring summary of the value of his talk to all of us in the audience.

The professional cleaner who gets plenty of jobs and gets them done but somehow never manages to make a profit has this same problem. When analyzed, his days have a familiar look. Preparation and finish-up don't pay anything. The revenue earned in productive time (actual doing) has to support and pay for this nonproductive time. Adequate preparation and careful finish-up are important, but only in proportion to the value of what is produced.

Your goal is to concentrate your time in the area where it will yield the most. If you can manage to do this, you'll continually gain time and multiply your accomplishments. Planning things, lining them up, assigning and adjusting them, and getting them started are all important parts of getting things done. But actually spending your time working on them is the big *uno*, the heart of doing.

Some officers of my cleaning company once had to drive to a nearby city for a business deal. They rounded up the right company car for the trip, some nice CDs to play on the way, called ahead for dinner reservations, checked the weather, coordinated their attire, selected gifts for important contacts, set departure and arrival times, etc. Little was done for the meeting itself—the purpose of this whole excursion—and the meeting fell flat (but the trip was great!).

Be Sure You're Threshing, Not Thrashing

Thousands of years ago, we humans found a way to gain a lot of fine food from a few seeds and some work—we began growing wheat.

The ripened wheat was cut and brought to a central location where it was "threshed" by tromping, shaking, and beating, creating lots of dust, chaff, hulls, and straw. Hopefully by the end of the day there was a pile of clean grain, too—the goal. But sometimes the crews showed up on time and willing and eager to work and they tromped, shook, beat, and sifted until they were out of breath. They had piles of straw and hulls, but for some reason no wheat.

This is just as true today as it was back then—the mystery of the same efforts with such different results. Let's call the grain-producing process threshing, and the other, thrashing.

Thrashing: when there's lots of movement,
but nothing gets moved.

We are all experienced thrashers. One day we hit the workplace and take calls, fill orders, create programs, phone, fax, e-mail, consult, and at the end of the day we have a nice pile of "did" and "done" to show for it. The next day, we arrive at the

same time, spend just as long, are just as sweaty and loyal, but at the end of the day we can't find a single productive thing done. If this occurs once in a while we can just call it a "bad day." But sometimes that immeasurable thrashing seems to triumph over threshing for quite a while. Days have a way of edging into weeks, weeks into months, months into years, and years into a lifetime. We see even good producers fall into thrashing despite the fact that they are willing, present, and working. Somehow, routines and real wheels are turning in the mill, but missing the grain.

Thrashing and getting paid for it is eventually disastrous, as both boss and employee will soon cease to survive without effective product.

What happens is simple. When we aren't pushed or pushing ourselves, we add five or ten minutes of trivia onto a call, a letter, a trip, a conversation, a meal, a break, a decision. If we average thirty tasks/operations a day, without even noticing we can use 300 minutes thrashing—that's five hours! Shaving and adding a tiny bit here and there adds up to a big chunk of time by the end of the day. Be sure you're threshing, not thrashing.

Don't Be Deceived by "Busy"

Busy is almost always perceived as a positive, a word we should respect. We almost always buy "busy" as an excuse not to talk. But all it really says is that someone is engaged in something. I've seen busy sleepers, busy time-wasters, busy loafers, and busy thieves—"busy" can be engrossed, totally occupied, hard at it, and not helping the cause or accomplishing anything at all. "I'm busy" doesn't say a thing about productivity or value. It only says there is some kind of activity going on. I clipped this congressman's report to his state on his "busy"-ness:

Working with You for Idaho

If someone were to ask me to list my priorities as your representative, I would put staying in touch with you at the top of the list. Whether it's meeting with sugar beet growers in the Valley or INEL officials in the Falls, I can best represent my district by maintaining close contact. Idahoans want, and clearly deserve, accessibility to their congressional representatives. Based on this commitment, I would like to give you a brief accounting of my trips to Idaho last year:

- 118 days in Second District
- Visited 5 senior centers
- 406 hours on planes, in airports
- 29 trips to Idaho
- Conducted 6 town meetings
- Visited 10 schools
- Visited 11 weekly newspapers
- Gave 2 graduation speeches
- Attended 7 Courts of Honor
- Presented 9 U.S. flags
- Spoke to 10 Chambers of Commerce
- Met with more than 500 individuals in district

And equally important, I maintained a voting attendance record in the House of Representatives of 96 percent.

This list of visits, meetings, presentations, hours at airports, etc., didn't really say what the congressman had done, nor did it indicate any worthwhile accomplishment. Attendance isn't an automatic asset.

When you pay out more than a million dollars in payroll every month like I do, you get really focused on results. My employees look at their checks to see how much the amount is. I look at their checks to see how much they did to get it. Some people do a lot to get theirs, and other people, on the same job with the same everything else, don't do a great deal. I pay either way and so of course I'm always looking, teaching, and leading to increase the number of super-doers working for me.

Almost no one sees himself or herself as deadwood or a lesser doer, of course. Many think that if they put on a uniform and show up, that's what counts. Well it doesn't—doing is what counts. This isn't only true of the business world, either. It's equally true at home, in a community or church organization, and in the most mundane daily personal chores and duties.

FOCUS ON THE RESULTS and fill in the blanks	
_____ is of no value if	_____.
Dieting	you don't lose weight.
Rounding up	you don't bring home any cows.
Overhauling it	it doesn't run afterward.
Planting	nothing grows.
Making sales calls	you don't sell anything.
Saying "Lord, Lord"	you don't live right.

Don't tell me how hard you worked—show me how much you got done!

Mental Alertness Will Up Your Production

In the early days of my cleaning business, I had two different fellows working for me, one named Barnes and the other named Max. They were about the same age and in many ways seemed similar. No matter where we worked or on what type of job, however, Barnes seemed to get almost twice as much done as Max. The quality of their work was the same, but Barnes was just much faster.

I'd watch them work and there never seemed to be a stride of difference, yet at the end of the day, Max had only achieved about 50 percent of what his fellow worker had. This intrigued me until the day it was all made clear. We were "dry cleaning" the ceiling of a large supermarket. Max, Barnes, and four other guys were lined up on the planks, scaffolds, and ladders all working at full capacity. Max's dry sponge (a special soft rubber sponge used for jobs like this) finally wore out so he jumped off the ladder and walked briskly over to the supply of new dry sponges. He picked one up from the box, removed the wrapper from it, walked briskly back to the ladder, looked around to see where he left off, then began working stroke for stroke again with the rest. A few minutes later Barnes's sponge gave out and he too slid down the ladder, walked briskly over to the box, and picked up a sponge. But then he *unwrapped his sponge as he walked briskly back to the ladder, and as he was climbing the ladder, he was looking to see where he'd left off.* By the time he reached the top of the ladder, he was working. The business of getting another sponge and getting back to work took Barnes thirty seconds and Max sixty. Why? Because Max wasn't mentally awake. **He didn't think about the next thing he had to do until he was in position and it was time to do it.**

Likewise, at our last company meeting, about a hundred managers and their spouses attended. The catering company set up a nice self-service buffet on tables on each side of a ten-foot hall, and the line passed by the first table getting main dishes and baked potatoes and toppings, etc., then reversed by the other table for salads, rolls, desserts, and juice. To speed up the line, which was dragging a little, I took up juice duty, filling and handing each person a cup as they finished filling their plates. I couldn't help noticing that some people went through the line taking the same things as others, but they did it twice as neat and twice as fast. Others held up the line for at least five minutes, picking and placing and deciding. Since I knew the basic business efficiency of each of them from their weekly and monthly reports and balance sheets, it began to be almost humorous. Almost without exception the laggers were the low producers in the company, and the ones who whizzed through were the star performers in the profit arena. How did they do it? While waiting at one of the tables, they were already looking over at and deciding about the offerings on the other. The slow ones, on the other hand, just poked and dreamed until they got there, and then they faced the decisions of white vs. wheat bread, spinach vs. Caesar salad.

I increased my carpentry and building speed 30 percent by learning to be awake when I worked. Before that, I always had trouble locating my tools minutes after I used them. Every time I turned around I was spending ten minutes looking for a pencil or wrench or measuring tape I "just had." My small son was so impressed by this routine that he used to slip in behind me when I left to answer the phone and hide a tool. Then when I started looking for it he would find it and receive much praise. It was months before I caught on to him.

The crowning experience, the one that caused a commitment to change, was the day I was behind schedule and knew I had used my hammer but couldn't locate it. I decided it was my wife's fault and went storming up to her to see what she'd done with it. After I made it clear that she'd lost my hammer, she asked me what I had in my hand. There was the hammer . . . and the epitome of mental laziness.

As a boy back on the ranch, making those long rounds on the tractor, I'd often become hypnotized by the hum of the motor and the warmth of the exhaust on my feet, and mentally I would fall sound asleep. It was always then that disaster struck. I'd hit a rock ledge or an old half-buried stump at full speed and rip the plow apart.

It's great to daydream and fantasize, but don't let it cloud or crowd you out. You won't believe how much faster you can absorb and accomplish things, and how much less repair work you have to do, if you just stay mentally awake.

Turn in Your "Hunting" License

This seems almost ridiculous to write and perhaps to read, but already today I'll bet you've searched for something for the tenth or hundredth time: wallet, checkbook, rings, watches, keys, stamps, eyeglasses. Not being able to find something we want or need—tools, clothing, papers, addresses, phone numbers, information—turns the next twenty minutes (or half the day) into pure unadulterated unproductive time. I know excellent, fast-working carpenters, for example, who lose two hours of the average eight-hour day rummaging and hunting for their tapes, hammers, clamps, etc. Wouldn't you say we spend about 10 percent of our lives looking for things? So if you reduced this even by half you'd be astounded by how much more you could get done.

Hunting through junk always undoes us emotionally, too. De-hunting your life is one of the biggest benefits of dejunking—see page 22 in Chapter 3. De-clutter and get rid of all that stuff you don't want or need (the stuff that smothers the things we *do* need). Then:

1. Have a clearly established parking spot for all your tools and projects.
2. Put them back when you're done with them so they'll be there the next time you need them.
3. Mark or label them—in BIG letters.

When I was building houses or clearing land, I used to spend about a quarter of my time looking for tools I'd carried off, laid down, leaned up against something, or half buried. (They camouflage themselves very cleverly once on the ground.) Then I got smart. Ten dollars' worth of bright red or yellow paint on the handles gave instant location and identification of all those tools if they were lost, left at the neighbors', or borrowed by someone.

Keep Things Convenient

A young man took a job painting highway stripes. On his first day, he painted ten miles of stripes; the second day, five miles; and the third, one mile. On the fourth day, the boss called him in for a "talk."

"You're fired!" the boss said. "You were doing fine at first, but now. . . ."

"I can't help it," the young man explained. "Each day I get farther from the paint can."

Make sure your key tools, tasks, and people are always within reach, even if you have to rearrange your workspace. Long distances put even high producers at a disadvantage.

Laying out your office, shop, kitchen, or yard to reduce the time it takes to process and handle things is an obvious way to increase your productivity. Even simple things like having the wastebasket close by, or lowering a counter or finding a table to exactly fit your height, can make a big difference.

Sometimes we get faster and better only to have the extra time consumed by poorly located items. We lose speed whenever we lessen convenience. Keep all your active projects, especially, fully accessible. Then, even though you're working on one thing, you can easily jump to something else if your mood or priorities change. If the others are open, exposed, in sight at all times, you can contribute to them or pick them up in a minute and run with them.

Keep Yourself Available

Notice that high producers always seem to be available. Availability can even outdo ability! Yet just when some people are getting their act together, beginning to be real go-getters, they get an unlisted number, a more remote office, three hideouts, and twelve assistants to screen them from everyone and everything. Or they go off to do so many things, so often, that no one can ever catch up with them.

No one can help you in life if he or she doesn't know that you're alive! If you are out of work, for example, should you just sit around reading want ads? No! It's better to be out actively looking and *doing*—even free or volunteer work if nothing else—so you can be observed and discovered.

If you want people to call you, you'd better not have a busy line—it's that simple. If you really want to do business, then you'd better put not only your office but your home and cell phone numbers, as well as your e-mail address, on your business card. People need to be able to find you to use, hire, or help you. If you're going to be in business, then be *at* business, where the clients and customers who are supporting and building you can reach you. If you've asked for customers, you've got to be there or quickly findable when the shipments arrive or service calls come.

It's true that you often have to get away from the mainstream to get something done, but you need to be available, too, on your terms and time. You don't need to stand in the street or the office with a "see me anytime" sign around your neck. Instead, provide clear and controlled avenues through which those who need or want you can get the message to you quickly—and then you can respond according to the value of the need or event at hand.

Quit Stalling Before Starting

A while ago, my editor and her assistant compiled the following list of some of the endless ways would-be writers can find to delay getting on with the job of writing.

You've already:

- Changed your T-shirt to a sweatshirt (or your sweatshirt to a T-shirt)
- Put on your slippers
- Cleaned your glasses
- Reset your watch
- Loosened your belt
- Trimmed your nails
- Scratched your head
- Washed your hands again

- Studied your profile
- Checked for gray hairs
- Washed your face
- Combed your hair
- Reinspected your freckles
- Brushed your teeth, put cap back on tube, rolled tube up neatly
- Fed the dog
- Let the cat in
- Made a snack
- Looked out the window
- Ate your snack
- Checked the fish tank
- Brought in the mail or paper
- Put the dishes away
- Made coffee
- Poured coffee
- Spilled coffee
- Cleaned up the spilled coffee
- Read the cereal box again
- Weighed yourself
- Cleaned the light switch
- Adjusted the lamp
- Cleaned your keyboard keys
- Dusted the monitor
- Emptied the wastebasket
- Practiced a new signature
- Adjusted the height of your chair
- Filled the stapler
- Checked the paper supply in the printer
- Inspected the watermark on the paper
- Played with paper clips
- Picked the paper clips out of the rug
- Lined up your erasers
- Gone through your e-mail inbox

- Played computer Solitaire
- Straightened your papers
- Sharpened your pencils
- Emptied the pencil sharpener
- Called your mother/grandmother/aunt
- Selected a CD or radio station
- Alphabetized your CD collection
- Put Dewey Decimal numbers on all your reference books
- Done your sit-ups
- Dusted the top of the bookcase
- Looked through the junk mail
- Perused the L. L. Bean catalog
- Balanced your checkbook
- Made that tune-up appointment
- Cleaned out your notebook
- Re-prioritized your old list
- Typed a new list
- Straightened the pictures on the wall
- Emptied your pockets
- Read the captions under the pictures in the dictionary
- Read a few old *National Geographic*s
- Matched all your socks
- Put all the hangers in the closet facing the same way
- Put a fresh box of baking soda in the fridge

There's probably nothing left to do but write . . .

If this seems familiar, it's because we are *all* artists at stretching out the start of something when we want to. This is called stalling, piddling, or—my favorite words for it—"twinking" or dinging. Under any name, it is a real time-waster.

If you want to see a quick increase in your productivity, just make sure all your time on a job or project is *working* time. Most people hunt, muse, head-scratch, daydream, pick up things and put them down again, etc., for about half of each hour they work.

Leave Yourself a Starting Place

Even the most disciplined of us sometimes has trouble getting started. So when you have to leave something partly done to be picked up again later or at some other time, always leave an easy starting place. Leave things ready—the bins full, the buckets handy, the clothes laid out on a cold morning, the car filled with gas the night before. Make sure the tools are sharpened, mark the place in the book so you don't have to search for it, write the number to call by the phone so you can make the call instantly instead of pausing to look it up.

Leave things neat and organized, too. Straightening up a mess at the start might technically take the same time as it would to clean things up the night before, but the mental effort of facing that mess before starting *will* delay the starting of even the best producer's project. Sorting things out all over again when you arrive is a real bummer compared to being able to pick things right up and start making time the minute you get there.

Get Moving—It Will Motivate You

A large rock was uncovered during an excavation project and seemed glued to mother earth. Five people attempted to remove it with crowbars and shovels until they were drained of energy. They lost not only their head of steam, but all desire to even attempt it further; not an ounce of muscle, will, or ambition was left in the lot. Even lighting the fuse on dynamite sounded like too much work. So like most "immovable" tasks, it was "tabled until tomorrow."

As the workers were all wearily packing their lunch pails and putting on their coats to leave at quitting time, one of

the workers, taking one last look, saw a little ledge that would serve as a perfect fulcrum. He set up a lever and applied a little push, and that massive rock *moved,* just a little. A movement, any movement, meant it could be done and was being done! All five flung off their coats and for the next three and a half hours, without a break or a drink of water, they wrestled with that rock until they removed it, and then went home humming and refreshed.

You too have observed this all your life—how mood can speed or stymie a job that needs to be done. The problem is that we usually wait for our mood to be just right, or until we think we have the ideal conditions, or until the time is convenient, and then we go for it. The "perfect" time for something comes about one time in 100, so we drift and wait through the ninety-nine others.

But movement is what *makes* the mood. So get started! **Once you're started you are indeed half done.** All producers live that motto. You own your moods and make your own convenience—"ideal" is, for the most part, manufactured—it's not a gift from nature. Just make a move and your mood will change. Waiting for your mood to change so you can change the world is like standing in front of a jar of peaches waiting for the lid to come off so you can partake of them.

Use Hot Times for Hot Projects

While I was still in college, someone told me that studying in the morning was three times more efficient than at night after work or just before you go to bed. I tried it and was flabbergasted. Thirty minutes in the morning beat three and four hours at night. I could read and write and memorize more and faster and remember it longer. It was much, much more efficient; it took less time to get the same thing done.

Doing the less taxing mental and physical jobs at night, on the other hand, is actually fun, and it winds you down perfectly for bed.

High producers pick and use hot times for hot projects! Don't allow low-fuel jobs to burn any high-fuel time. Don't file, address envelopes, or read mail or magazines when you're fresh and keen. High producers do trivial things during trivial times; they never use prime time to trim their cuticles.

I bundle up all those little things that require reading or response—letters, forms, questionnaires—and when I hit a time, such as on the plane or waiting in the terminal, when my body has to be there but my mind is free, I do them. Never in prime working hours, or when I'm with my kids or spouse. (I've even been known to take care of a few detail chores during dry sermons. . . .)

Ship-Jumping

High producers are often asked, "Where do you get the energy and ambition to do all that you do?" After all, it's easy enough to get discouraged, bored, tired, and impatient with just one project. Well, guess what. The go-getters also get discouraged, bored, tired, and impatient—they're human just like you and

subject to exactly the same emotions and psychic forces. That's why they have multiple things going simultaneously.

This approach can be called "ship-jumping," in that when a project or task starts to drag or becomes uninteresting, or hits a snag, you can jump ship, leave it, and go do something else. We all do this somewhere. When you've been lying in bed or standing in line, or in the same position too long, and your arms and legs are cramped, you shift your weight, stretch out, curl up, roll over—anything to break the bind, and boy, does it feel good.

We only have so much endurance, both mental and physical, for any one task, and jumping ship is a great way to keep going with other tasks. Just be sure, if you're going to be a ship-jumper, that you have a big fleet, so when you leave one ship, you have another to board immediately. Lots of people quit a project, or fail at it, and then just lie around and go stale. Doers quit and leave projects too, probably more than anyone else. Their secret is that they have forty others (fresh, new, and interesting) that they can leap onto. Then an hour, a day, or a week later, when that one gets dull and they begin to get bored, they can jump ship again.

When my wife and I go to Hawaii for two months or so in the winter, everyone assumes that we're just resting up from a busy and demanding year. When we leave Hawaii, however, we've not only further perfected the model low-maintenance house we built there, we've usually accomplished fifteen or twenty other major projects and hundreds of minor ones in those two months. Yet we still did rest and enjoy all the exotic sights and sounds.

Hawaii is a place where the body says "I'm sleepy" or "I'm hungry" often, and if I had only one or two things or nothing to do there, I'd eat and sleep the whole two months away. But eating and sleeping is only so rewarding, so I spend the entire time jumping ship. What ships do I jump? Well, besides that low-upkeep house, I have the four or five new books I'm always working on, plus a pile of other projects to choose from. One year I built a volcano (with a hidden storage building inside) out of lava rock. Other years, I made a set of steps down into the jungle, a huge rock-and-block fence, and a scary *Raiders of the Lost Ark* bridge. We're always planting new trees and bushes and adding new highlights to our nature trail. And I'm always happy to help the neighbors out when they're painting a house or putting up a garage.

So there are plenty of places to go when I jump ship. I work my rockwork projects when it's cloudy, because that tropical sun shining down on those black rocks could cook you. Instead of fighting it, I go into the shade and plant a tree or two and weed the ferns for an hour or so till I get bored. Then I grab my machete and head for the cool edge of the jungle and hack back the overgrowth for an hour, and when the rains come I go into the house and work on one of my books. When I hit writer's block, instead of beating my head against it, I shift to another book and let the first one simmer a while. I type, and when my brain waves seem to be starting to waver, I switch over and write by hand. After three hours of intense authorship, instead of forcing myself through three inefficient and uninspired hours more, I switch to something else like clipping and pasting art ideas, doing some layout, designing a new book cover—just keep flowing. When I'm feeling drowsy, I run out and heave some giant rocks around or form up and pour another step into the jungle, lugging 120-pound buckets of cement around to get the old blood pumping. Or make a clearing, move stumps, or smooth the driveway with my tractor. If it rains again, I go fix tools, or go in and write again, or do an interview.

If you work this way, you'll be fast, efficient, and motivated, not only refreshed but highly productive, because at all times you can assure full concentration on and commitment to what you're doing.

Sometimes, when things are flowing, I'll write and type for six or eight hours without ever getting up. As long as a project is rolling, stick with it. But when you start waning and drifting and getting mushy, don't quit or beat on yourself— jump ship. You'll see lots of different things progress and get done, and be able to really savor them. It sure beats the one-at-a-time routine, and it's amazing how it all adds up. In three months of just random and catch-can working, I've completed 300 feet of trail, 100 feet of fence, twenty feet of steps, all of a volcano, and written four new books, plus I've done dozens of media interviews!

Stay aboard only as long as you're enjoying the ride. When you reach the point of stalling out in your production, you'll know it, so change—do something else or just go to bed if you have to—to revitalize yourself.

> ## Can You Get More Done When You're Mad?
>
> I doubt it. Mood affects all productivity—and the worse the mood, the greater the likelihood of bad judgment (even if speed picks up). We can't go around waiting for the perfect mood to complement our agenda or spending tons of time psyching and re-psyching ourselves up. Real producers handle the mood liability by having many projects, jobs, and duties lined up all the time. Then they can simply jump ship to the one where the juices are flowing. When one gets boring or too hard to take, leave it for a while and tackle the one you're in the mood for.

How to Switch Smoothly from One Job to Another

To avoid any time lost "changing gears" here, do it all in your mind before you actually stop and change what you're doing. An hour or so before you quit pouring concrete and go back to your desk, or before you leave your desk to go pour concrete, make the transition and start organizing the next task slowly in your head. This way you're always in gear and in full swing when you get to your new assignment. You don't have to stand or sit in front of it for fifteen minutes psyching yourself up.

Do It Now and Perfect It Later

Lots of us whine and worry and even punish ourselves when we aren't quite 100 percent pleased with our progress or by the outcomes of some of our projects. Just remember that none of us can do everything well, and rest easy because all through life you'll find that expediency generally outdoes perfection. A savvy advertising executive told me something once that I've found to be true in almost any endeavor:

> You can get more accomplished by getting something
> done, even a little rough, than polishing and procrasti-
> nating it indefinitely. Do it the best you can with what
> you have, and get it out there, where you and others can
> see and comment on (and criticize) it. You'll reach your
> goal faster this way than by working forever somewhere
> off by yourself, stewing away and trying to mold and
> perfect something by the book or by the anticipated
> reaction to it.

No producer ever whimpers about not being very good
at something. Producers may know that they aren't good at
something, and not even know how or when to do it. But if
it has to be done, they launch into it and then melt down the
bullets they dodge to redo and rebuild it as they need to. Some
of my best stories, scripts, and other accomplishments have
been the result of feedback on far-from-perfect trial balloons.
Often "rough cut" not only gets the ball rolling but ends up
good enough to make the cut!

Facing It is Easier Than Fearing It

The expression "I'd rather face a firing squad than face that"
is almost literally true for many of us at times. After we've
conquered the majority of obstacles to our objective, there are
always two or three we've held out till last. They're the really
nasty things we would rather not have anything to do with.
(Example: The committee appoints us to tell Joe Higgins
that the job he has held for twelve years is to be taken over by
someone else.)

Unpleasantness comes along at times of victory as well as
defeat and at any time it is unwelcome. People have resorted
to lying, cheating, and stealing to avoid facing something
really unpleasant.

Many good businesspeople capable of excellent compre-
hension, accurate bidding, and efficient job operation have

failed because they disliked and avoided a few minutes a day of the unpleasantness of paperwork. Unpleasant obstacles, if you attempt to ignore them, will not only sabotage you, but rob you of mental and physical energies.

When the interstate highway was being constructed in our area, it had to be built right through the mountains. Even in a situation like this there is some soft going, but sooner or

later comes an unpleasant "thump"—solid rock—and the contractor, like us, has to face it. He can work around those rocks for a while, but before he can make real progress, they have to be blasted out. The contractor has a commitment, a contract that specifies where the road must go.

The contractor can't afford to procrastinate the extraction because he will be penalized, and the same is true of us. He loses money—we lose precious time. We can easily forfeit many hours of time and energy dreading, worrying about, postponing, and trying to decide what to do about unpleasant tasks. The five or fifteen minutes it takes to finally face many things will be much less painful than five hours or five days of anticipation agony. Sometimes the agony of anticipation is so long and intense that an unpleasantness never is faced, so we suffer guilt for the original failure to face it, as well as the practical consequences of that undone thing.

So what it is the secret of facing up to things like this? Direction, again. If you are committed, you have no other choice. This eliminates that "getting up the nerve time" and just gets the job done. Your commitment doesn't remove unpleasantness; it merely forces you to deal with it. Then the unpleasantness generally is removed, and the relief and freedom that follows is high-octane fuel to boost future achievements far beyond anything lost in the facing.

Make Sure Everything Around You WORKS

What's worse than finding the shovel handle split when you feel like digging, trying to start a dead lawn mower when it's time to mow, or struggling along with scissors that won't cut? Think of all the things you own right now that don't work. What good are they, not working? They have to be fixed sometime and that time always ends up being when you need to use them *now*.

Broken or poorly working things, dull, half-functioning tools always ruin other things—including our temperament when we try to use them. They slow you down, and never allow you to be a real go-getter. Fighting a sticky window or drawer over and over isn't very productive, and breaking it while fighting it is even less so.

Here's one of the easiest high-production principles to put in practice: Don't own anything that doesn't work. It'll let you down at the worst possible time (it's cold, dark out, you're already late, etc.). The job won't get done, and you'll lose not only the time and dignity you spent fiddling with the tool, but also your train of thought and concentration for hours afterward. This very day or week, repair or get rid of anything you have that doesn't work (changing or replacing relationships that don't work may take a little longer). **If it doesn't work, fix it, change it, clean it, restore it, dump it, sell it, or give it away.** It's better to have no jack at all than one that won't work.

If it won't work, not only does it lack value, but you also waste a lot of potentially productive time waiting around and whimpering about it, tinkering with it and trying to fix it. Its potential to malfunction will guarantee you trouble, and it adds ten things to your mind that you don't need.

This Fix It or Flush It rule isn't just for tools and machines—it's for habits, procedures, bookkeeping systems, and promises—anything that doesn't work.

Preventive Maintenance

"Breakdowns" instantly convert a productive activity into an unproductive one. The time and money lost usually can't be recovered, and breakdown can mean delay, and sometimes injury or worse—even death.

One of the best business managers in the country looked like just another ordinary Idaho person to all his colleagues.

Yet he led the national productivity index year after year for what was at the time the world's largest company. Nothing seemed to go wrong for him; his output was the highest and his expenses the lowest. The motors in his 120-vehicle fleet lasted longer, and he got 20,000 more miles out of their tires than anyone else did. His building maintenance costs were lower, phone installation times, repairs, and other costs were lower, too.

What was his secret?

> I've learned an art called preventive maintenance. When I (or any of my employees) have free time, instead of standing around waiting for the next thing to happen, I analyze the age of the products in service, thus determining that in the next year certain items will be worn out. Then, while everyone else is waiting for a problem to occur, I promptly change the old piece or product (which I'll have to do anyway). This not only eliminates the later replacement, but also the incoming complaint call, dispatching repair people, checking in and checking out.

He serviced, rebuilt, and restored machines and buildings before they broke at the wrong time, and corrected and counseled employees before they quit or had to be fired.

This man, a smart operator, also consistently won go-kart races (a family hobby). He and his sons had the same cart as all the competitors, but would beat them time after time. The secret again: Preventive maintenance. "How come your cart doesn't sputter and quit once in a while?" others would ask. The answer was easy: During the days and weeks when there wasn't a race, the man and his boys spent a few minutes maintaining things.

A popular piece of advice we hear is "Don't fix it if it ain't broke." That's as silly as saying, "Don't change or replace tires until they blow" (and wreck your car, put someone in the hospital, make you late for an appointment, etc.).

We can't predict or foresee the exact moment when a worn belt, frayed piece of wiring, failing motor, cracked tooth, or withering friendship will finally give out. But if things are kept in good repair and maintained ahead, we do have some measure of control and protection against chaos and interruption. Some people may be impressed by how efficiently someone is able to round up all the cows that get out. I'm more impressed by the person who never fails to close the gate or fix the weak spots in the fence.

Preventive maintenance is just as important (if not more important) in the home and in human relationships as it is in business.

How to Deal with Down Time

We can't control traffic or other people's moods, never mind the universe, the government, and all those viruses and twists of fate out there. So no matter how organized or sincere we are, there comes a time when our driving gear is thrown into neutral.

Waiting in line, for example, can be classified as "down time," as can other little unwelcome events like lost luggage, no-shows at work or appointments, something lost, something breaking down, or a sudden attack of illness or depression. Because it generally isn't our fault, most people accept down time. We assume that when down time strikes, you stop, wait, criticize, daydream, or otherwise just idly sit until you can proceed as before. But super-producers don't handle down time the same as average folks. They use it, well, and *now*. They sure don't wait until down time happens and then figure out "something" productive to do until it goes away. They have better plans, and I'm not talking about reading—we all know enough to carry something to read in case we get stuck. These days, the majority of to-dos, including the paperwork we all have so much of, can be done in down time.

I've put out more than thirty books in the last two decades, and right now I'm working on more than forty new ones. The majority of these were conceived and written while I was gaining my million-plus miles on the airlines or riding in a car somewhere, or waiting in lobby lines or for delayed meetings, or while others were on coffee breaks.

Refocusing is an easy thing. When you're hit with down time you can draw, diagram, take pictures, write, plan, call, clean, dejunk, fix, exercise, converse, sing, etc. There are phones everywhere, and we all have briefcases or car trunks. You can easily carry paper, pens, books, and other tools right with you at all times to give you a week's worth of things to do on the spot anywhere, if you need it.

How much precious time with your children or romantic time with your mate has been sacrificed to something that could easily have been done in a down-time situation? Right now assemble a big pile of "do when I'm derailed" projects and carry them with you or keep them handy. You'll be amazed how much more of your prime time can then be spent for prime things in life.

Chapter 8

The Healthy Stretch
(Will It Hurt?)

As budget projections, measurements, expectations, and results were being tallied in a great organization, all centered around how much each person and division could be expected to do, one man stood out in the midst of them. He had the most productive and quality operation, the most satisfied customers and by far the most motivated workers; he spent the least money, and he had the lowest number of failures in all departments. When his awestruck colleagues asked him how he did it, he gave a one-sentence answer:

> **"There is only one way to run this operation—overworked and understaffed!"**

Heresy! Slander! Exploitation!

Was he ruthless and insensitive? He sure wasn't. Remember, he was speaking from a strong, proven position—not just the best work and highest profits, but also the happiest people. Let's see what he was really saying. . . .

Haven't we all said or heard 100 times:

- "I'm running as fast as I can now."
- "I'm working as hard as I can already."
- "I'm carrying as heavy a load as I can."
- "I'm keeping up with the rest."

Who is it that sets the gauge or standard for how much we can do? Do we compare ourselves with what others have done or are doing, statistics, or what our boss or parents or teachers ask of us? Do we calculate how much we can and should do by comparison or contract, or are our production goals geared to our capabilities, as they should be?

No one in this world is just like you. (I think that is the most profound, stimulating, and motivating bit of information ever.) No one, out of all the billions of humans, is just like you. In fact, no one is even close when it comes to thoughts, feelings, and abilities. So why do we always use what others do, or what we're told or assigned, as the measurement of peak performance and production capabilities? Your own capacity—mental, physical, emotional, and spiritual—is the only assigner and regulator of how much you can do.

Never measure your potential by what others are doing. Only you know what you can really do. No one is an official "go-getter"—that's just a label lying around for anyone willing to fulfill what he already knows deep in his heart he can do.

"I'm running as fast as I can" or "I'm carrying as much as I can" doesn't really tell us anything, because most of us have never really tested ourselves enough to know how fast or how much that is.

"I'm only one person" is irrelevant, too, because one person—a real producer—can do more than 10,000 others and have 10,000 rewards and blessings for it. If you're really interested in how much you can do, then forget all the facts, figures, and fictions, and those figuring out "fair workloads" and rest ratios, and charts and tables establishing a "norm" for you!

To get a better picture of potential, when you feel you've peaked in your production on something, go watch a real professional do it—skiing, diving, shingling a roof, gardening, sewing, singing, painting, bricklaying, raising kids, cooking, writing, anything you like or want to do. **Go watch a pro and you'll marvel at how fast and well they do it.** When that "wow" of admiration shivers through your bones, remember that there are always possibilities of doing even more and better than what you see. Never envy a champion, an expert, or a number one; don't covet their prowess. Because they are exceptional or awesome at the moment doesn't mean that you are less or bad, only that you have a greater capacity to do than you are presently taking advantage of.

That's the key to being a great producer: realizing and being convinced that you have almost unlimited ability. Forget the comparisons. They just keep temporary scores in life and provide fuel for idle conversation. It's the realization and attainment of your potential, your dreams, desires, ambitions, and feelings that counts.

We've all shot a contemptuous glance at the idiot who reminds us in a loud voice while we're in agony: "NO PAIN,

NO GAIN." One fellow I knew said that to his wife in the final hour of childbirth, and it nearly cost him his marriage. Gain doesn't necessarily take or make pain, it only asks us to stretch a little, and do it often. Anything worthwhile puts on a little strain and leaves a few stretch marks on us. You don't have to hurt to do more, you have to hustle and lengthen your stride.

"Workaholic"

We see this label every day and some of us have it applied to us regularly. The implication is that you're some kind of hyper weirdo if you put in long days and really love the work you do.

There are people out there telling us to slow down and do nothing but relax. I would confidently challenge all these consultants and advisers with the fact that top producers of our society—the "workaholics," if you will—are actually less neurotic than the average, run-of-the-mill man or woman. All the "workaholics" I know are enthusiastic, positive, healthy, and mentally and physically energetic. They use fewer pills and stimulants, can appreciate play and relaxation better, are more generous with their time and money, and are more sensitive to social and human needs (and do something about them). You don't hear workaholics whimpering nor do you see them standing around with their hands out for rescue. So if you fear that becoming a top producer might move you into the "workaholic" league, rest easy. It would be the best promotion you ever got!

Afraid of Burning Out?

The modern fear of "overload" or "burnout" is almost humorous. There might be some "bore outs," "bum outs," or "fade outs," but burnouts? Most people's flames aren't even lit yet, so how can they burn out? How often do you hear someone say, "I'm just burned out, I'm ready to quit/ change/retire." The problem isn't burnout. Their flame might be out, all right, but not from overproducing. More likely the flame starved out for lack of fuel—lack of doing and the rewards of doing.

Burnout has become a respectable label for quitting or slacking off. That magic word is supposed to excuse us from creative laziness, not eating or sleeping wisely, and lack of consistent production. **Burnout (with some rare exceptions) is 90 percent cop-out.** Most of those who say they've run out of gas have run out of guts. It isn't production or work that burns people out; it's just the opposite. Actual accomplishment doesn't burden and burn you out—it ignites and inspires!

In our modern American society, far more people die from overdrinking, overspeeding, oversmoking, and overplaying than from overwork. You can stop worrying about working yourself to death, especially if you are producing anything, because productivity shapes you up rather than wears you down. Why do we always blame "work" for what ails us? Most of us are lucky to have a job to get us away from what can be real beater-downers—leisure and luxury. Too much to do is usually motivating, because coping with it requires the most intense personal application, loyalty, ingenuity, sacrifice, and service. These requirements stimulate and build—not burn— a person.

How many great athletes, entertainers, or executives burn out when demands are high and they are producing? Few! Their results refuel, revitalize, and rejuvenate them. When we're working at maximum rpms, when our efforts are in greatest demand, the exact opposite of burnout usually occurs—it's called *regeneration!* Productivity brings life, love, and renewed energy.

Don't Push Yourself?

Don't listen to all those people who say, "Don't push yourself." Most of them don't have any push themselves.

During my senior year of college, my wife and I were ready to find our dream place. For us that meant something rural, and our search led us to a small sixty-acre farm nestled in a green valley between majestic peaks. An old man who was unable to walk and his son, a severe diabetic, owned the place. In his younger years the old man was known for his fine raspberries and strawberries, and he had picked this place as the perfect spot for the final fulfillment of his farming. He planted lots of berries, drilled a well, and planned out an elaborate irrigation system. The well turned out to be a dud and failed to produce enough of a flow to fuel the sprinkler lines. In spite of this, when my wife and I looked at the place, the berries were blooming. A neighbor told us how this was possible. "That old man fills a five-gallon bucket and crawls up and down the rows all day, watering the berries by hand and smiling."

He sure didn't feel perfect, but he was getting near-perfect results, as well as deep satisfaction and admiration. As I work and run this same place today, sometimes with a sore back or an aching foot from arthritis, I'm still inspired by the original owner's example. Even restriction has a high gear!

Production Is Often the Best Cure for What Ails Us

My mother told us a story when we were young about a pioneer woman with four small children. The woman was bitten by a rattlesnake. There were no easy ways to make contact for help, and her husband would be gone for four months on a trapping excursion. Knowing that if and when she died, her children would also perish alone out there on the plains, she quickly forced herself to make bread, prepare all kinds of foods, and fix up the house so as to assure the children's survival until their dad got home. Ill as she was, she worked feverishly and unmercifully, and instead of dying, she lived through it. The doctors told her later that all the activity and perspiration, etc., had helped her rid her body of the poison and the work saved her—and the kids.

I never knew whether this was a true story or not, but it did a great job of bringing home the point that work is good medicine for much of what ails us. "Down," "tired," and dispirited can be sweated out of you!

We'll often (if not always) have something wrong with us somewhere. Instead of waiting around to be cured, you can use production as a cure to help make you feel better. Lots of us with a full day planned find ourselves feeling yucky that morning—we have a cold, a headache, we're tired, "out of it," or in some other condition that says "let it go for now." Real producers say, "Nonsense." Often if you just brace, bandage, or bundle up and go to it, you'll find yourself operating on all cylinders before noon.

No time will ever be picture-perfect for production, and so many of our "yucks" are mental, not physical. We all know plenty of professional sick-leave-takers; they seldom are producers. The people you know who "never get sick" do get ailments like all the rest of us, but they'll tell you, "Well, no use lying in bed feeling miserable, I might as well be on the job, accomplishing something."

What they forgot tell you, however, is that they don't really feel that miserable on the job once they start to produce. They feel needed and responsible, see things coming together, and hate to miss anything . . . and all of this sweeps illness into the background.

Lou Gehrig, one of the greatest producers in baseball, played more than 2,200 consecutive games without a miss. When he was x-rayed after his death, it was discovered he had had seventeen fractures in his fingers (some had been broken two or three times). He'd never said a word. A broken finger is pain galore, never mind trying to catch screaming throws from third or gripping a ball with one.

A champion stays in the game and plays on, hurt or no hurt. **So instead of grinning and bearing it, grin and do it.** If you're going to be feeling awful anyway, you might as well be working. Accomplishment is one of the few things that can take the focus off pain; it's one of the best remedies for it. And we can often work and accomplish as well or even better when we're feeling under the weather—whereas attempting to just "enjoy ourselves" or attend some recreational event when we're feeling down and out is a lot harder.

Production isn't a single-position proposition. If you are prevented physically or mentally from doing one job, you can adapt and do a different job, take on a different part of the job you were on, or do your regular job differently.

"But if I Work Too Hard I Won't Be Able to Smell the Flowers . . ."

Once you're under suspicion of being a workaholic, the famous quote "Take time to stop and smell the flowers" will be presented to you more times and in more ways than you can imagine. Cards, notes, letters, calls, earnest conversations, and even threats will come your way from well-meaning associates, urging you to relax and be sure to savor life before it goes by. But dedicated doesn't have to mean dull.

Have you noticed that the people who try their hardest to smell all the flowers are often the ones who miss the choicest blooms? Those who actively hunt for adventure have little or none, and those who are forever talking about and seeking relationships have few.

The best way to absorb the sights, sounds, and scents of life is while covering and cultivating all the ground of production and involvement—learning, risking, building, doing. The one who makes it all happen—who plants, grows, and weeds the flowers—really savors the flowers, not the person who merely views or sniffs them while passing by. The rewards of service, sacrifice, and accomplishment will fill your soul with a sweetness no flower could ever muster. The memories of a creation made or a job well done or a life changed for the good will reward and sustain you longer than the finest and most lasting aroma of a rose.

I once took forty Boy Scouts to a Jamboree. We passed some of the most beautiful parks in the world on the way, and because I was busy supervising the boys' activities the entire time, no flowers got sniffed by me on that trip. That was years ago now, but the satisfaction of having made some small contribution to those young lives has permeated my being ever since. It delights my soul far more than the finest gardenia ever could.

I've lived in the midst of mountain pines and alfalfa fields, and smelled exotic blossoms from Europe to Alaska, Hawaii to the Arizona desert. I've loved and benefited from it all, but working long and hard to improve yourself and serve others is still sweeter. And it will give you twenty different life-long rewards instead of just the pleasure of sniffing the same familiar flower twenty times.

Work, the Ultimate Recreation

Have you ever thought of high production as a restorer? If you equate doing a lot with getting tired there may be a secret here that you've been missing all these years. The reason high achievers have lots of energy and can put in unbelievable hours is because doing is generally more restful than not doing. Doing is less stressful than waiting, weighing, dodging, brooding, wondering, and wandering. Lounging lights no burners in the human soul, but accomplishment does.

|||||||||||||||||||||||||||||||||||||||||||||||||||||||||||||||||||||||||

Most people's idea of entertainment is golf and dinner or going to some show, instead of making your own show and feasting on something different than what a restaurant can provide.

|||||||||||||||||||||||||||||||||||||||||||||||||||||||||||||||||||||||||

In the early days of our marriage, for example, my wife and I had our hands full. I was getting my cleaning business underway and averaging ten to twelve hours daily on the job, and she was finishing up her degree and caring for our first four children. And we were building our first house. After long, hard weeks like this, one Saturday morning I was getting things cleaned up around the shop when an unexpected $150 arrived in the mail. I called my wife excitedly and told her—we were really going to enjoy ourselves tonight. But we weren't going to attend a party or go out on the town. That would be a bore. By 4:00 P.M. I was on my way home with some cinderblocks, an "I" beam for the door frame, and some cement and lime. (We could only build our home as we could afford to purchase things.) By suppertime we had butterflies thinking about having the whole kitchen wall on the house finished. We would get the kids to bed early, set up the lights, mix a batch of mortar, and lay blocks and beams until 2:00 A.M. or so. Out in the beautiful evening air, geese honking, frogs chirruping, nighthawks whipping through the sky, owls calling in the pines, and our own house going up—what fun! We ended up a lot less tired than if we'd sat through a late show or an evening of conversation.

Producing—doing something worthwhile—is rarely "work." It's usually restful and relaxing because it's so rewarding. Covering ground may get tiring, but gaining ground isn't!

The Biggest Secret of Accomplishment: Time on the Job

I hired an eager college student once who was thrilled with the job, the pay, and the schedule. One week later he quit. What was the reason? In his very words: "Work takes up all the time on the job."

"What?" I asked, "I'm not sure I understand you . . ."

"The work I have to do takes up all my time while I'm there."

"I still don't understand you, man."

"Well, Harry, my buddy, has a job over at the college plant and he reads gauges and makes one round every hour, and then he can sit and study or read or watch TV and get paid for the rest of the time. That's the kind of job I have in mind."

This represents not only a trend, but a general attitude today. The result is that we're all spending less and less time actually working and more and more time sick-leaving, training, traveling, breaking for coffee, committee-ing, unpacking and packing up tools, showering, and forty other things. Diving into, hanging with, and staying with a job for hours and hours is getting to be so rare, the people that do it shine forth like a second sun! The early rock n' roller Buddy Holly never wore a watch and friends would ask "How do you know when to stop?" He answered simply, "When I'm through."

High accomplishment: Seldom is it the result of talent, skill, luck, or better equipment; much of it is just putting in longer hours. Lots of adults retain the childhood attention span. We fiddle with something for a few minutes and if the rewards don't start bouncing in right away, we drop it. High production comes with serious time on the job. I'm asked hundreds of times a year, "How do you get so much done?" I'd like to say "I'm a magician, I just presto it done," but the main answer is just plain "time on the job." Sitting down at the computer at 5:00 A.M. and not getting up until 3:00 in the afternoon (not even to eat or go to the bathroom); staying down in the field or at the shop or behind the counter. Amazing how much of a time management expert this will make you—just being there doing, working, thinking, and banging things out, swinging the hammer, wielding the pencil or the mop—how good an organizer you become and how much gets done!

Most accomplishments, doing great things, take time. We're such an instant society today—thirty-second soups, fast-drying paints, quick oil changes, pushbutton entertainment, etc. We tend to think everything comes in the blink of a computer chip—not so! Things are accelerated today, but production takes time. To accomplish, you've got to be on the job, hour after hour, day after day, not out to lunch, or constantly on vacation.

Often you'll ask someone what he or she did today and you'll hear about the project he or she worked on, but for some reason didn't finish. When you total up the time actually spent on this project during an eight-hour span, the person really only worked two hours and the other six were spent hanging around, not in and on the job. The person kind of worked out of the corner of his or her eye, and didn't hit the project head on. There is so much to do, so many attractive and distracting things going on, especially around home. We can jump from one thing to another very easily and remain on some so briefly that at the end of the day we really haven't spent any time at all on them.

You've got to put in the hours on something to get it done, period. You can't just flash back and forth by it. The chief difference between success and failure lies in the single element of staying power. It takes a long time to get to work and get ready; why not keep at it for twelve hours for a change? I'm not asking you to be a fanatic, just to stretch a little.

Though few virtues run second to endurance, in sticking with a project or cause and overcoming any obstacles or opposition you can reach a point in all this when you realize you are not headed where you want to go, and all of your options for changing the situation or circumstances seem depleted. When this happens, don't go further or deeper into undesirable territory. These are the times when jumping ship (see page 155) is smart; waiting until you have to abandon ship is usually a waste of time.

The Magic of Momentum

Watch the super-producers, those who seem to get twice or three times as much done in a day. They capitalize on the magic of momentum.

They know that one of the real secrets to high production, winning, and genuine go-getting is that once you're really going and making headway, you don't stop. When the spirit is willing, your imagination is expanded, and creativity is pouring out—keep moving. Don't take a break, go to bed, eat, or anything, even if "it's time" to do so according to your usual schedule. Spontaneity is a source of great progress.

> When things start going your way, then is the time to turn on the rest of the burners. Never coast or halt or go to bed because you're ahead!

When you have things going, when you're in the groove, everything is rolling. Don't stop and bow for applause, just go for it. When things are moving, don't stop to read your press or evaluate your progress. When things are falling into place

and you are feeling like you could go on forever, do so. There are times to ignore the clock, meals, nags, even tired muscles, and just keep going to the finish line. Make it a marathon. Meals, breaks, rest sessions, and any other unyieldingly scheduled events are for people who have nothing else to look forward to. If you're scoring, keep scoring, even if you are ahead of "them," "it," or your old record.

Notice that when an athletic team gets on a roll, it seems almost unstoppable—even poor teams can crush bigger and better teams when they're on a roll! Then what does the losing team do to quell their opponent's progress? They call a "time out" to let the momentum cool down and most of the time it works perfectly. Likewise, people starting to really move on an idea or project can become so proud of and impressed with themselves, they take a little time off to celebrate and guess what? They can't get back in the swing of things—it often takes days, or they just plain lose it. We all know that once you overcome inertia and get something big and heavy going, it becomes easier to move. If you let it stop, getting started up again is murder, takes ten times the effort and energy, and often you can't even get it going again.

When it feels good, go for it—don't stop, look up, or turn around to assess. As Kenny Rogers told us, "There is time enough for counting, when the dealin's done."

Think of Pressure as Positive

Start down a row of workers and ask, "How do you like pressure?" The first one will roll his eyes and grasp his throat, the second one will say, "Stress and strain." The third one will duck, the fourth will say, "I hate it." But keep going and suddenly one of them will brighten and say, "I love it!" and she means it. Odds are that the "love it" one will be the top producer of the bunch!

Pressure is usually thought of as bad or negative these days, but think about it. Pressure means things are moving fast and pushing hard. Pressure means something worthwhile is being done: a lawn is being watered or a spectacular geyser is going off, or a diamond is being formed deep in the earth. We couldn't get along without blood pressure, tire pressure, and water pressure. Pressure is like a cast on your arm or braces on your teeth—we sure don't like them when they're on, but we love what they do for us in the long run!

Pressure might have a "do it or else" ring to it, but we need some of that in our lives. Eighty percent of the negative kind of pressure is caused by us, anyway, not by our employer, loved ones, or school, as we always imagine:

- "Boy, the teacher really has the pressure on me." The teacher gave you an assignment three weeks ago and you waited until today to start working on it.
- "The boss sure has the pressure on me." She expects you to produce for your pay, and if you haven't been, you are the true cause of the pressure.
- You're in the closing seconds of a ball game, and it all depends on your next hit or shot. The pressure is indeed

on, and who caused it? You volunteered and signed up for the team and the pressure potential came with the package.

P.S. You don't work *under* pressure, you work *with* it! Pressure is a plus if you're in front of it—it pushes you up and on. If you're under it, it pushes you down.

An Ironing Lesson

People wonder why the super-producers often spot and start to develop several new projects while buried and busy with thirty other ones. Four of my best books were conceived and started during the breathless finish of six others. You just cannot put off inspiration or delay opportunity. You need to not only strike while the iron is hot but keep your other irons warm while you do. It can be done if you are really convinced that what you are doing is worth doing.

Move It!

So many people seem to believe that if you do something quickly, it isn't as good as it would be if it were done slowly. When I used to tell people I could paint their entire house in one day, they'd gasp in horror—it always took them or others a week or so to do it. "How can you do a good job if you do it so fast?" would be the very first question. Technically, the faster that houses are sanded and primed and painted, the better. Lengthening out the job lets moisture into the bare wood and you get weathering, checking, dust, and insect residue between coats. The same is true of many of the projects and assignments we undertake in life—delay only deteriorates the end result or makes the job harder.

"But it takes time to do anything right"—Says who? I've seen people clean as fast as a streak of light and their work was perfection, and plodders who took forever to get through an area, and it didn't look much different when they were finished. Don't make the assumption that something done well has to take a long, hard time. Things can be done fast and well.

Go-getters go. You don't have to dart like a hungry squirrel around tourists, but hop to it. Running, trotting, leaping, jumping, and hustling are virtues. They're impressive to watch, they're motivating, and they set a good example for onlookers. Moving fast is stimulating for you, too, and above all it gets a lot done. When TV advertisers sell us cars, antacids, or pizzas, notice that the products are always moving fast, working fast, and being delivered fast, respectively. Who in this world today wants slowness in things or people?

Race the clock instead of watching it! I run instead of walking most of the time—it's fun—and I notice others often start running then, too! Humans, like horses, have four speeds once you get past stop: walk, trot, canter (hustle), and run. There is a time and place for all of these on most journeys and duties, but if you'll start and pattern your life from the high end (run) on down, you'll get a lot more done and be much more successful than if you're always starting from the low end of stop or walk.

There is a woman in her late forties who does odd jobs and errands for me. I knew before I hired her that she has always been admired as a doer, and once she started working for me I understood why. As soon as she had the job or the item to be delivered in hand, she ran, and I don't mean that metaphorically; she actually sprinted like a miler when the situation merited it. It seemed strange to see a middle-aged woman running at full speed, and it sometimes embarrassed her husband and children. But everyone who worked with and around her said "Wow"—and gave her more work—mainly because she hit it all on the run.

This might be an extreme case, but hustling is better than ambling or strolling through your assignments. Dashing is more dashing and healthy and productive.

Don't Let Weather Decide Whether

The handsome young man describing his dedication to his sweetheart was raving forth with promises: "I'd swim the widest river to see you, I'd fight dragons and demons, I'd walk through deserts, just to kiss you. I'd climb Mount Everest every day if you lived there, I'd run through a forest fire to get to you. . . ." Now nearly out of breath with such unbridled affection, the young man started out the gate, turned, and said, "See you tomorrow night, Honey, as long as it doesn't rain!"

Far too many of us play this fellow's game, letting weather or circumstance be the deciding factor in even our most passionate commitments.

Hot, cold, wet, dry, windy, cloudy, in the mood or out of the mood, whatever—if you're going to be a producer, it's irrelevant. A real producer can't wait until it's convenient, or circumstances are just right, before he or she moves or acts. If it's cold, then wear a coat; if it's record cold, then wear two; if it's so cold that no human should even consider it, then carry a hot water bottle under three coats, but *do it* if you've planned for it.

No one can plan for all the possible weather or circumstance changes, and for sure we are going to hit lots of foul and unfair weather. If something like this happens, go for it anyway; be tougher or take another road, but don't let setbacks or rain showers shut you out of a job. There can be real agony in doing more when you're doing it under adverse or negative conditions, especially when all the slackers aren't out in the storm with you. But when the sun comes out, you'll be the one on top.

But I'm Having a Bad Day!

I was fourteen and it was a great morning. I bounced out of bed to dress, but couldn't find a shirt and then one of my shoelaces broke when I was putting on my shoes. I headed out to the barn for a ten-minute milking job, and the cow took off and ran to the far end of the north forty. I chased her for forty-five minutes, and lost my new pocketknife in the process. By then I'd missed the school bus. That meant I'd miss two tests, and my brother didn't show up after I called him to bail me out. Then the cow broke the stanchion. In haste now to "catch up," I spilled the three-gallon bucket of milk on the flowers, which alerted every cat around, and they tore up the bed trying to get the milk. It wasn't even 8 A.M. yet!

About now something more serious happens at times like this: We come to the conclusion that this is going to be a bad day. Things are already off stride, behind, and limping. Our momentum hasn't just stopped—it's in reverse. We're going in the hole! So we move into a panic mode, begin to rush, hurry, and find out just how true that old saying "haste makes waste" is! It seems everything waited until this important day to get you.

What do high producers do with bad days? Oh yes, they have them—in fact, they have them more often because big doers have more things lined up and crowded in. So when something goes off the rails, the chain reaction is bigger and nastier! Interruptions, breakdowns, stalls, screw-ups, and delays are all part of the picnic of life. What's the best way to deal with them?

First: Don't let what's still ahead be ruined by what's behind. Most bad days start out as just one or two setbacks, and then *we* end up making more innocent duties go bad. A tire can't be changed easily, so we kick and punch it, injure our hand, dent the car, break the lug wrench, and offend onlookers with our language. **Producers never stew or storm more than a couple of seconds.**

True, you can't control the elements, or some of the people you have to work with, or some of the situations they create. But you can control yourself. Don't let yourself be undone for the day by a little discord.

Second: Never announce it to everyone: "Hear ye, hear ye, hear ye all . . . I'm having a really bad day." This just serves to convince you and others of it, too. Then they'll help you find more bad news to fulfill the prophecy.

||||||||||||||||||||||||||||||||||||||||||||||||||||||||||||||||||||||||||||||||||||||||||||

High producers prepare for a rainy day with big, current project lists. Then if they're dropped to the ground by a bucking horse, or have to lay low to evade a tornado, they can switch to the ground-level stuff on their list.

||||||||||||||||||||||||||||||||||||||||||||||||||||||||||||||||||||||||||||||||||||||||||||

Third: Set the lost, broken, or damaged aside if you can. There is seldom time and space in the already established schedule for the time and cost of restoration. Insisting on doing it now will break your momentum and affect the whole series of imminent or coming things. So gather up those broken or scattered parts in a bag and shelve them (and go back and patch things up at a better time).

Fourth: Your frontlog is healing ointment for even the worst wounds. Have a lot of "to dos" handy at all times—not just outlines and schedules, but what you actually need to accomplish those want-tos, ought-tos, and better-dos. Then, when a goodly part of today's agenda goes bad, or a big delay or interruption comes, you won't have to just wring your hands. You can tackle one or two new assignments instantly and never miss a beat.

Bad days are perfect ship-jumping times (see page 155), and they can end up better than what you scheduled. The secret is having enough choices to fit any situation.

Those Five-Cylinder Days

Some days we just aren't firing on all pistons, mentally or physically. We find ourselves sputtering, lunging, jerking, or dragging through the day or week, sometimes even the month. Well, lurching along at a broken speed is better than just lying down and waiting for a mystic healing of the soul or stiff muscles. Movement mends most things better than anything.

On that big frontlog of yours (that you are carrying everywhere with you) there are plenty of five-cylinder-level jobs and projects. Match them up with your current output and you'll progress and accomplish while you're down—almost as much as when you are up!

Body and brain rarely sag at the same time. Learn to bounce when your brain goes dead—dive into a blood-pumping physical duty until your muscles are making refusal motions. Then when the body tires, lie down and think, read, write, plan.

If You Hit a Slump . . .

In the best-planned weeks of mice and men, regardless of market and demand, schedule and priority, there comes to high and low producers alike: the slump.

You seem to be stuck on dead center, all your faculties seem to fizzle out on you, and no matter how hard you flog away at it, you can't do anything right or fast. The more you fight this, the worse it gets; your sales go down or your timing is off. Fear not; even the best hitters and the highest producers have their slumps.

Instead of getting all excited like a bug that flies into a house and knocks against all the windows trying to get out, land somewhere for a minute or two. Refresh yourself on your objectives and the reasons why this situation might be upon you.

When you get into a slump, you can jump ship (see page 155). Go to another, easier, more appealing or urgent project and let the one you've stalled on sit for a while. It's amazing, when you get away and stay productive in another avenue, how the project left alone for a few hours, months, or even minutes comes back into focus and gives you a firm grabbing place when you get back to it. Switch! That's why it's always good to have lots going on so you have lots of options and choices.

If You Feel Like Giving Up, You've Almost Reached the Goal

Remember, the give-up point is often just before the accomplishment point. You'll be frozen to the bone by 11:30 if you know quitting time is noon, but if you have to hang in there all day without a break, you won't get cold to the bone till 4:00. It's the same with hunger and thirst. If you know eating time is 1:00 P.M. you gear for it and are famished, starved, and ready to sprint to the table at 12:30. If that same morning you know you are going to miss lunch, you'll be a little hungry, but won't let it bother you until later that afternoon.

If you learn to walk ten miles, you aren't tired till the nine-mile mark. If you are walking five miles, you'll be exhausted at the four-mile mark, and if you're walking three, you'll be dragging at two and a half. Remember this when you're setting goals and listening to your own complaints.

Are You Sure You're "Too Tired"?

For many years, in the last hour or two before bed, I would convince myself I was too tired to do anything but flop down and suffer through a night movie or flip through a magazine. Then, I started pushing myself just a little. When there was zero mental and emotional energy left, I picked a menial task (like filing) and pushed myself to do it.

On a road trip one day, after thirteen grueling hours of mental and physical effort, I got back to the airport so worn down from lack of sleep that I slurred my words and stumbled on my way in. I had a five-hour flight to Salt Lake City ahead of me, and surely I could do nothing but sleep on it. By the time the plane took off I was frozen with fatigue, and tried for thirty minutes to drift off, but those seats and arms pushed at me from the back, the front, and the sides, making any real slumber impossible.

So I pulled out a legal pad and some books and notes, and forced myself to start writing. Within minutes two pistons kicked in, and then four more ignited, and by the time we landed I had twenty pages of the best stuff I'd ever done.

As we've all discovered when circumstances suddenly change, "tired" is as much mental as it is physical. Ever seen a tired fisherman when the fish start biting, or a sagging athlete when the play is thickest? A slow-moving mother when a child is in danger? Give me an exhausted person on a Friday afternoon, who is dead on her feet, used up, doubtful if she'll live until 5:00 P.M., and drop her in a slot where suddenly something critical depends 100 percent on her. You'll see a rousing, restored, still-ready-to-go dynamo!

Don't be afraid of being tired. Lots of wisdom and commitment comes to you when you're dog-tired. You'll recover, and if you've done good hard work to get tired, the sleep that follows will have the best healing power you've ever experienced!

Expect Some Wounds with the Wows

My granddaughter Kristen, age ten at the time, on productivity: "I know I did a lot today because of the bumps and scratches." What an original measurement!

During the 1988 Jamboree encampment of 32,000 Boy Scouts, our single troop of thirty-eight Scouts led the entire assemblage in cuts treated at the medical tent. Those nicks from busy knives seemed less important when someone toured our camp and saw the unique artistic walking sticks each boy made (and all the others envied). We led the entire encampment in other kinds of woodcarving, too.

The guy who moves the ball the most in the game will get beaten and tackled the most, and the woman who does the most at work is often the target for the flack of the fifty people standing back and being average. You have to carry the ball or go to bat to gain ground or score runs, and there are just more risks in the front seat than the back. Bruises, bumps, scratches, hurt feelings, even injustices are no strangers to high producers. It's part of the production package. Wounds are part of the price of winning. If you can't accept this, you'll seldom see production.

As you pull closer to the speed limit, you're going to blow a few tires and burn up a motor or two, and you might even offend a person or two, but all heals or can be fixed. The pleasure of producing is balm for the worst wounds. Few of those scuffs and scrapes will show or be long remembered, but your accomplishments will—they'll end up standing out and rewarding you and others.

For sure, **the destination is worth the jolts of the journey,** so never hold back on doing because it might hurt a little. You'll get an unbelievable payback!

Will You Be Ignoring Others if You Do a Lot?

Another illusion many people have about "doers" is that they are so single-focused that the rest of the world and its people may be tuned out. The exact opposite is true. The very act of building something (a case, a house, a plan, a kingdom) is rooted more in generosity and love than in selfishness. Most doers spend little time in purely self-gratifying pastimes and often spend little money on themselves.

The claim or worry that in the rush or push to achieve, you don't have time for anyone is also way off. Production requires a great deal of interactive communication and sharing with others, including family and associates. Building is social, not solo. The many people involved in the process of accomplishment are part of what motivates super-doers to do more.

When you are doing, many others are in the process with you, and being expanded by it, which makes production a blessing for all of those involved. People who share an enthusiasm are already in the loop, and the others usually have open invitations to join in the fun. And people who work together bond more strongly and longer than people who play together. Everyone who participates in a project owns the outcome. On the home or business front, it is "us," not "me," that usually benefits from the bottom line of all those efforts. Often our accomplishments are, in the long run, ways of looking after and loving our neighbors, and using our talents and assets to do it.

When I wake up in the morning, my first three thoughts are (and have been for as long as I can remember):

1.   What can I do to change the world for the better today?
2.   Who can I do it with?
3.   How can I best get the chores out of the way to get to the more productive, creative things?

The ABCs of the Healthy Stretch

A. **Ten Cows Are Easier to Herd than a Single Cow**
The question most often asked of a go-getter or highly productive person is, "Boy, you sure have a lot of things going. How do you keep track of and take care of them all?"

The answer is one of the biggest secrets of accomplishment. It may sound crazy but it works perfectly, it's been proven over and over again. Multiple things don't always mean multi effort! Ten cows are much easier to herd than one single cow. Several children are easier to manage than a single kid. The reason is, the others or extras around help take care of the one. Having just one goal, job, project, or activity going is about the most awful and inefficient thing I can think of. Real producers never let themselves get in that position. They'll start up and have twenty or thirty things going at the same time.

Notice how even when a high producer is buried and nearly overwhelmed with work—he or she will always take on another giant project!

Observers may think high producers are crazy when they do this. Mothers-in-law will whine about it, reverends will shake their bony fingers about it, specialists issue columns of warnings, but the go-getter has discovered something they haven't—that extra job is just ammunition to help get all the others done. The extra job never adds work; it only cooperates and accelerates.

You can easily do as much as—and probably more than—most of the go-getters you are envying right now. Thinking that you can only do one thing at a time is like saying you can only have one friend at a time, love one child at a time, etc. You are capable of doing hundreds of things at a time, and it will put a beauty in your life, not a burden.

B. Fish with Five Hooks on the Same Line Doing things on the way to doing something else—fishing with five hooks on the same line—keeps your brain alive and people impressed with you, and best of all, your productivity up.

I've employed tens of thousands of people since I began my first business, and many of these people have worked in "the office," where they are blessed with about fifty times the assignments as those in field and floor work.

Administrative assistants are one of those types of office workers that really get the brunt of an extra workload. On the surface, most of the assistants we had were about the same: They were all eager, fast-moving, helpful, and loyal, and they all had about the same office skills. But some could produce about twice as much as the others.

The standout quality these "double-doers" had was the ability to do things on the way. Whenever they got an assignment, they would make, on paper or mentally, a pick-it-up-or-do-it-on-the-way list. Then they would route themselves so that on the way to their destination and back, they could stop and get several other things done. This took almost no extra time and saved another single-purpose trip later. Most women are experts at this, and the more children, jobs, responsibilities, interests, and hobbies they have, the better they get at it. They ultimately become more efficient than those they work for or with.

How many times do we go right by something to do? The key is staying aware of what needs to be done, when, and where, while working from a frontlog. The rest is just a matter of reading maps. Making a special trip to do something utterly mundane is a boring chore we can all happily do without.

C. Stay on the Front Line Heroes and champions are made in the battle, in the game, and on the front lines. Where there is risk, injury, buffeting about, and opposition, there is also usually the greatest productivity.

The American Dream is about personal freedom, but being free from responsibility and accountability isn't having it made. Usually, it's just the opposite: personal bondage! We work, scheme, stick our neck out, and sacrifice to achieve financial independence—so we don't have to answer to anyone. What happens when most people attain "it"? Marriages fail, spirituality lessens, health deteriorates, enthusiasm evaporates, charity disappears, and attitudes sour. On teams and staffs, in families and organizations, the front line is where everything is happening. It's where life, knowledge, and action abound, where the seeds of greatness are sown, sprouted, and harvested. When you insulate yourself from the action of the front lines, you cut yourself off from the very things that make you grow and prosper and make you productive.

So step out in front, where you're on the hot seat to produce and perform and be accountable. The good life isn't luxury—it's the ability to produce! Be where you have to answer, speak, give, and deliver!

If you want to prove yourself, then you have to keep yourself on the proving grounds, stretched to and even beyond your capacity.

Chapter 9

The Rewards of Getting More DONE (Every Day!)

When we find ourselves getting more done every day and week, as Jackie Gleason said, "how sweet it is."

The best salespeople I've ever seen are those who don't ask for your money or even a commitment, they just talk you into taking the product for a no-obligation tryout. If the product is good, the selling is over. You want and are willing to pay. If you could leave your old watch with the dealer and wear a high-producer's watch for a while—one that makes twenty-four hours seem like forty-eight (because you're getting twice as much done in a day!)—you'd never return for the old one. You wouldn't even ask for a trade-in, because now you would have all those extra hours, plus new accessories not on the old model:

1. Endless selection of opportunity dial
2. Bonus builder
3. Benefit compounder
4. Leadership hand
5. Energy igniter
6. Help-soliciting beeper
7. Vice-buster switch
8. Greatness gear

Your new watch will have so many hidden buttons to bless your life, it'll be like the latest computer. You'll probably never even be aware of all the wonderful built-ins that will help give you that good life you've been after.

Where Is Opportunity?

Right on the job! When you're about your business, on the job, doing what you're supposed to do and doing it well, it's amazing how many good opportunities come your way.

So many people go out and seek their fortunes by making sales pitches, sending business cards and brochures, conducting mass e-mailings to potential clients. That's the hard way to grow and produce. If you're out actually working—painting, cleaning, fixing, successfully performing your job

for other clients—many people will come by and see you, your truck or equipment, and your skill. Before long, they'll wonder if and when you can come and do the same for their house or them.

No matter where I am, keeping busy eighteen hours a day—either with my own personal or business projects or community or church undertakings—is the best way to relax and rack up rewards. When I was building a 300-foot-long rock wall on our property in Hawaii, there were unending rewards from being on the job. Working out there in the sun and air, with all the birds and the view, was the most enjoyable experience imaginable. I got good exercise, was really accomplishing something, and when the fence was finished it would increase our home's value. The fence was also along the road and neighbors, tourists, joggers, hunters, horseback riders, and the like were constantly going by. That simple fence job, not counting its cash value and the personal enjoyment of just doing it, yielded:

- A mason stopping and teaching me some new bricklaying skills
- A college curriculum director buying one of my cleaning courses
- Beautiful people stopping and visiting
- People sharing fruit, food, invitations, ideas, and conversation with me

It was amazing. All of this came free and extra as I was working. Had I gone looking for any of it, I wouldn't have found even half as much at half the quality. Being *on the job*—on location, in action—drawing pictures, digging, singing, or dancing, just doing whatever you're there to do—will yield some of the most productive results imaginable. At no cost or effort on your part, it'll all come naturally. Productivity is a natural attention-getter! It will work for you.

Production Always Brings Unexpected Bonuses

One of the youthful experiences I remember best is hunting time, not so much the hunting itself as the uncles, aunts, cousins, and other guests who would come to hunt. Cary Grant, Bing Crosby, and Gary Cooper even came and hunted on our places! I got to know the habits of the wily pheasants pretty well because when the big people were hunting I was the unarmed "busher," or the guy who would cut through the thickets and flush the birds out. Good bushers hit every pocket hoping for a reward, and generally the more pockets of wheat, willow, and ditch bank you walked through, the more pheasants.

One day I saw a big fat rooster pheasant run into a clump of bushes and he didn't come out the other side—a sure chance to bag a bird. Uncle Oscar said, "Go in there and get him." And being a good go-getter, I went tromping into the clump and it exploded—pheasants jumped up everywhere, it must have been a national pheasant convention. Thirty or forty pheasants flew out of that single little thicket, while I was just after the **ONE**.

Such are the lessons, the laws, and the rewards of production—when you're doing one good thing, not even looking or asking for anything else, **something extra and unexpected will always appear.**

A friend of mine at great effort and expense took up mountain climbing to learn to climb and enjoy it, which he did, but as he mastered the peaks, other talents came forth. He developed muscles; he conquered fear, learned to make quick decisions, and discovered new strengths and sides to his personality. He found new friends and saw new country. Mountain climbing was the thing he went after and got, all the rest were by-products—they just came along with it *free,* with no extra effort or planning.

All producing and go-getting does that for you. Most kids join after-school activities for fun—including a chance to spend time with friends and meet new ones, etc. But before they're through, they learn loyalty and honor, and how to earn opportunities and work on a team. They may also have a chance to travel and become acquainted with and maybe choose a career, while keeping themselves occupied with constructive things, and thus out of trouble. In other words, here too one pursuit brings a whole array of benefits in the end.

Another friend of mine was determined to learn to be a good enough dancer to teach it. It took a stretch—six nights of classes and practices a week—to learn and do this, but she did and she was good. And by the time she was done, she'd not only accomplished what she'd set out to do, and enjoyed herself and made a nice living, but also had friends throughout the western United States. In addition, she gained a love and understanding of music and met people from other lands and cultures. For the one thing she worked toward, she received twenty other rewards, for no extra effort or cost.

Years ago, my wife and I were in Hawaii for a brief vacation when we heard a request in church for people to go over to an ailing person's place Saturday morning to do the yard work. I got up early that morning (as good go-getters do) and went over with my shovel, pick, and jungle knife for a little workout. By noon I ended up with ten special Samoan coconut trees, a stalk of bananas, three new friends, two invitations for dinner, and another invite to go fishing. I also learned some things I didn't know about gardening, got acquainted with some new tools and five new kinds of plants, and got an out-of-print souvenir map of the Hawaiian Islands. Think of what I'd have missed if I'd just stayed in bed that Saturday morning. From two hours of work, more than a dozen spinoffs. I couldn't have done better if I'd paid for or planned it!

Those unexpected rewards from high production are what make for a really fun life. The producing itself is a turn-on and enjoyable enough, but when ten or twelve or even 100 extra things come along with it—and they do—it's like your birthday every day! Those little bonuses are part of the harvest for a go-getter, one more incentive to become a producer of the highest echelon!

There's something so exciting, so rewarding, so motivating about doing more and upping your output and expectations of yourself. You do more and touch more lives, thus enriching yours. It gives life some intensity for a change, and you make dust instead of eating everyone else's.

Don't we all want (secretly or not so secretly) to change our lives and ways of doing things to accomplish this? Well, I've found a shortcut to it: Just demand, outline, bite off, commit to, and *do* MORE—and BETTER. Quit accepting the level someone else has achieved, or the amount some hypothetical formula says you should be able to do. Living a "budgeted" life is about as thrilling as watching paint dry. Bite off a lot, and if you can't chew or digest it all, spit some of it out if you have to, and call the process "practice," not failure. You can do five safe, careful things a day with no mistakes or you can stomp and sprint around and do eighty-five things in a day and possibly fail at 50 percent of them. You'll still have accomplished thirty-five! And from the 50 percent that failed, you'll have gained respect, new relationships, and experiences. That's how we learn, and soon you'll be able to do eighty of the eighty-five with no failures!

Less Time to Get into Trouble!

Let's look at another side of it. We all spend lots of time fighting off temptation and problems. We have to exercise to keep in shape, be careful not to eat or drink too much, constantly discipline ourselves to stay on the ethical straight and narrow, keep honest and upright, and control our passions and desires. Hitting these things head on, day after day, is a rather inefficient, grinding way to do it. But when you're busy, or even overworked a little, going after all those opportunities to produce at work, at home, for church and state and your fellow humans, many of these problems either never confront you or take care of themselves, because you just don't have time for them anymore.

Think about it a minute: When you're out there really doing something—interested and challenged and committed—you're not lonely or bored, the work develops your physical and mental muscles, you don't have time to gossip, and there's almost no time or interest for trouble. **Free and idle time is what often destroys people's lives.**

A Navy admiral and psychologist I once knew was telling me about his work. Most of his counseling, he said, was dealing with breakdowns and the problems of the enlistees—drugs, drinking, emotional disturbances, etc. "Why?" I asked. "What is the cause of this?"

"That's easy," he said. "The culprit is '*free time*.' There are a lot of slow times, and times with nothing to do but wait in service life, and many people can't handle it. This is when they pick up smoking and drinking habits. When the effects of those wear off and things haven't changed, they do even more nonproductive things to pass time—get into drugs, fights, etc. They aren't bad people, just *un-busy!*"

All the wisdom and abilities you have won't do much to give you a happy life unless you use them to produce. Being a high producer is like having a big savings account. When disappointments and discouragement hit you (and they will), you'll be on top of the barrel, not at the bottom. So you'll have perspective and the resources to cope and even give strength to others.

Being a go-getter will even help you develop humility. Sitting around with lowered eyes or citing scriptures in a low voice is not humility, nor is it the way to achieve it. People tempered by the fire of fulfilling lots of assignments and failing at others, who are always struggling for great accomplishment, are the ones who really learn humility. It's another free by-product of high production. Few are more pretentious than the newly rich by accident or inheritance; contrast them to a person who has produced a lot under his own steam. The doers don't have their noses in the air, yet you can be sure they are confident of their abilities—confidence and an honest regard for self are unmistakable ingredients of true humility.

Would You Like to Be a Great Leader or Teacher?

Everyone dreams of being a great leader or teacher. But how do we actually go about attaining this? Neither education nor money nor position will ensure it—we all know plenty of people with all three who can't even lead their families or the people who work for them. Great leadership to change the lives of others will come through what you do and do consistently, not what you know or own. **When you develop the habit of doing, lives will be influenced all over the place and you won't even know it's happening.**

When I lived in Hawaii as a young man, I met a Japanese gentleman named George Kondo. He was a genuine high producer and he liked people; he lived to change lives. How did he do it? For years, he got up early every Sunday morning, went into his huge garden, and picked fresh flowers to sew up into leis. Then he took the leis to church or work with him and if anyone looked neglected or lonesome, George would present that person with a lei. If anyone looked hungry he'd invite that person home for dinner—he even invited total strangers. He did this, steadily and aggressively, for thirty-five years. When George began to travel around the country later, no matter where he went, he had friends and loved ones—many of them total strangers before the morning they met George and received a beautiful garland of flowers from him.

Almost fifty years later now, as I travel across the country speaking, all I have to do is mention my home in Hawaii, and many times people will come up to me afterward and ask, "Hey, do you know George Kondo?" They don't know the governor, or anyone else from Hawaii, but thousands know George. When George was in his eighties, bedridden at home, and my wife and I went to see him, we almost had to get an appointment. He (deservedly) drew caring visitors from all over the world—one of the just rewards of a real doer.

No one said it any better than Robert Baird, 1855–1916, in his hymn "Improve the Shining Moments":

Improve the shining moments;
Don't let them pass you by.
Work while the sun is radiant;
Work, for the night draws nigh.
We cannot bid the sunbeams
To lengthen out their stay,
Nor can we ask the shadow
To ever stay away.

Time flies on wings of lightning;
We cannot call it back.
It comes, then passes forward
Along its onward track.
And if we are not mindful,
The chance will fade away,
For life is quick in passing.
'Tis as a single day.

What Will Happen When You Become a Go-Getter and Start Producing More?

- You'll be in demand, instead of being demanded of all the time!
- You'll have more time than you ever had before. (And to think people try to find extra time by cutting down on what they're doing.)
- From now on, no matter what life serves you up, you can't be cowed or defeated. No matter what happens, you still have worth.
- You'll have joy in the morning—and something to get up for!

- When you get absorbed in purposeful production, success and happiness, all on their own, will sneak through a door you didn't know you'd left open.
- You'll know, maybe for the first time in your life, that you really matter. Having doubts as to whether you count—to your children, spouse, partner, boss, employees, or just in general as a human being—is one of the biggest sources (if not the biggest source) of unhappiness. If you know you matter, then adversities, setbacks, and discouragements are only temporary inconveniences and slight irritations that you know you'll overcome.
- When people are convinced that they make a difference, they make a difference.

Producers matter, and *knowing that you matter* is the biggest motivator in the world.

Produce! A Lot! All the Time! Start Now!

What would you do if you could get tons more done? Share more, serve more, lift yourself, be more selfish or unselfish? Once you have more time you could even waste a little time if you wanted—get out of survival and into savoring!

Do You Know Some Time-Multiplying Magic I've Missed?

What have you learned about the best ways to multiply accomplishments, speed yourself up, and overcome obstacles and interruptions? Would you like to share your knowledge with me, and the world of other productivity-minded people, in future books on this subject? Write to me at don@aslett.com, or P.O. Box 700, Pocatello, ID 83204!

Index

A

accomplishment
 as counter to pain, 174
 as motivator, 19,
  104–105
 as social bond, 192
 time on job as secret to,
  177–179
achievers. *See* high achievers
activities, average time spent
 on, 49
advice, sources of, 115–117
agitation, 41–42
associations, 122–123
automatic deposits, 132
availability, 128, 149–150
avoidance, 69

B

backlogs, 92–93
bad days, 185–188
beverage rituals, 44–45
big breaks, myth of, 102
burnout, 170–172
busy, vs. productive,
 142–144

C

catching up, 103–104
character traits
 of high producers, 11–14
 test of, 20
checks, 132
circumstances, waiting for
 right, 184–185
clothing, 37–38
clutter, eliminating, 22–25,
 148
coffee drinking, 44–45
committees, 117–118
communications equipment,
 110–111
computers, 47–48, 108–110
confidence, 80
consistency, 102

D

deadlines, 94
decision-making, delayed,
 78–80
dejunking, 22–25, 148
delegation, 105–107
deliveries, 131–132

demands, responding to high,
16–17
direction
choosing your own,
64–65
course corrections and,
74–75
importance of, 53–56
order and, 73–75
disharmony, 125
distractions, 26
down time, 165–166
See also relaxation
duplication, 127

E

early
fixing things, 95–96
morning hours, 93–94,
155
preparation, 89–91
principle of being, 85–100
eating habits, 34–36
effectiveness, vs. efficiency,
138–139
efficiency
vs. effectiveness, 138–139
through multitasking, 194
efficiency aids. *See* helpers
electronic banking, 132
elimination, as key to productivity, 21–25
energy, 56
errands
See also tasks
accomplishing via mail or
phone, 131–132
ethics, 135
excitement, 57–60

excuses, for not accomplishing
more, 14–16
expectations, meeting, 16–18

F

fatigue, 190
finances, taking control of,
30–31
fixing things, 95–96, 162–163
food-centered living, 34–36
free time, as trouble maker,
203–204
front lines, 195
front logs, 92–93

G

giving-up, 189
goal setting, 57, 189
go-getters. *See* high achievers
grooming, 38
group helpers, 117–124
grudges, 43
guilt, 43

H

habits, unhealthy, 31–33
See also time wasters
health
importance of, 31–33
work as cure for bad, 172–176
helpers, 101
example of super-doers as,
115–117
group, 117–124
peace, 125
spares, 125–127
tips for hidden, 124–135

tools as, 107–113
volunteers as, 113–115
high achievers
advantages of, 1–6
becoming a, 9–11, 100
character traits of, 11–14
as examples, 115–117
examples of, 11–18
help received by, 101
rewards for, 197–207
history, learning from, 82,
127–128
holidays, 132–134
hustling, 182–184

I

idle time, as trouble maker,
203–204
image, 37
indecisiveness, 78–80
injuries, 191
instinct, listening to, 82
intelligence gathering, 127–
128
interruptions, 26–30

J

jewelry, 37–38
job
See also work
enjoying your, 58–60

L

lateness, 86, 88–89, 97–99
leader, becoming a, 204–206
ledge, the, 103–104
lists, 65–67

lost items, searching for,
147–148
love, 5–6

M

mail, 131–132
maintenance, preventive,
163–165
meals, 34–36
mechanical output, vs. production, 6
meetings, 118–120
memberships, 122–123
mental alertness, 145–147
momentum, 179–181
mood, 154, 159
morals, 135
morning hours, 93–94, 155
motivation
accomplishment as, 19,
104–105
enjoyment as, 58–60
getting started as, 153–154
limited use of, 104–105
movement, as motivation,
153–154
multiple projects, 155–159,
188, 193–194

N

nagging thoughts, 42–44
noises, 26
nonproductive time, 139–142

O

objective, defining the, 137–138
off days, working on, 132–134

online banking, 132
opportunities, 198–200
order, efficient, 73–75
organizations, 122–123
overanalyzing, 77–78
overkill, 76–77
overload, 170–172
oversleeping, 45–46

P

parties, 33–34
past events, dwelling on,
  41–42
peace, 125
perfection, 159–160
persistence, 56
personal relationships, 192
pettiness, 44
phone calls, 131–132
planning, doing own, 64–65
play time. *See* recreation
potential, measuring your,
  167–170
preparation
  doing own, 64–65
  early, 89–91
pressure, as positive, 181–182
preventive maintenance,
  163–165
prioritizing, 25, 66, 67
procrastination, 162
production
  as cure for problems, 172–
    176
  vs. mechanical output, 6
  unexpected bonuses from,
    200–203
productive time, 139–140
productivity

affect of mood on, 159
increasing, through mul-
  titasking, 155–159,
  193–194
increasing, through organization, 148–149
lost, to misplaced items,
  147–148
momentum as key to,
  179–181
in morning hours, 93–94
reasons for increasing, 1–7,
  83
rewards of high, 197–207
secrets of, 11–14, 81–83
testing your potential, 20,
  167–170
projects
  See also tasks
  assessing value of, 68
  big vs. little, 68–70
  finishing early, 91–93
  finishing quickly, 182–184
  not perfecting, 159–160
  stalling before starting,
    150–152
  starting place for, 153
  switching between, 155–
    159, 188
  working on, with others,
    123–124

Q

quickness, 182–184

R

reading, 38–39
record-keeping, 30

recreation
  excessive, 46
  work as, 176–177
relaxation, 175–176
repairs, doing early, 95–96,
  163–165
reports, 30
responsibilities, delegation of,
  105–107
results, focusing on, 60–63,
  144
retirement, as waste of time,
  15
rewards
  of high productivity, 197–
    207
  unexpected, 200–203
rules, following the, 63

S
Saturdays, 132–134
schedules, 70–72
seminars, 120–121
setbacks, dealing with, 185–
  188
ship-jumping, 155–159, 188
shopping, 36
slumps, 188
social events, 33–34
socializing, controlling, 28–30
spares, 125–127
spare time
  making use of, 129–131
  wasted, 50–51
spectating, 47
stalling, 150–152
standards
  raising, 17–18
  working to, 70

status, 37
stress, from deadlines, 94
super-doers. *See* high achievers

T
tasks
  See also projects
  accomplishing via mail or
    phone, 131–132
  defining the objective for,
    137–138
  delegation of, 105–107
  efficient order of, 73–75
  low-energy, 155
  piggybacking, 132
  stalling before starting,
    150–152
  switching between, 75, 155–
    159, 188
  tools for, 107–113
teacher, becoming a great,
  204–206
television, 47
time
  assessing value and, 68
  budgeting, 72
  down, 165–166
  idle, as trouble maker,
    203–204
  logging your, 51
  maximizing productive,
    139–140
  spent on the job, 177–179
  spent waiting, 94–95,
    165–166
  travel, 128–129
  waiting for "perfect," 154
time efficiency, everyone is
  capable of, 9–11

time fragments, 129–131
time wasters
    beverage rituals, 44–45
    clothing, 37–38
    computers, 47–48
    delayed decision-making,
        78–80
    dwelling on past events,
        41–42
    eliminating, 50–51
    food-centered living,
        34–36
    grudges, 43
    guilt, 43
    image pursuits, 37
    meetings, 118–120
    nagging thoughts,
        42–44
    overanalyzing, 77–78
    overkill, 76–77
    over lifetime, 49
    oversleeping, 45–46
    pettiness, 44
    play time, 46
    rubbish reading, 38–39
    searching for lost items,
        147–148
    shopping, 34–36
    social events, 33–34
    spectating, 47
    stalling, 150–152
    waiting, 94–95
    worry over noncontrollable
        events, 39–41
to-do lists, 65–67
tools
    duplicate, 127
    as helpers, 107–113
    keeping convenient,
        148–149

    nonworking, 162–163
    preventive maintenance of,
        163–165
travel time, making use of,
    128–129
trivia, 39–41
trying, as opposed to doing,
    81

U
unhealthy habits, 31–33
    See also time wasters
unpleasantness, fear of,
    160–162

V
vacations, productive, 135
value, assessing, 68
visitors, controlling, 28–30
volunteers, 113–115

W
waiting time, 94–95, 165–166
weather, 184–185
work
    See also production
    as best medicine, 172–176
    as ultimate recreation,
        176–177
workaholics, 170, 175
workplace, portable, 128–130
worry, over noncontrollable
    events, 39–41
wounds, 191